New Ideas in Card and Paper Crafts

New Ideas in Card and Paper Crafts

Graham Airey Ben Bates Ian Price

Van Nostrand Reinhold Company

New York · Cincinnati · Toronto · London · Melbourne

Van Nostrand Reinhold Company Regional Offices:
New York Cincinnati Chicago Millbrae Dallas
Van Nostrand Reinhold Company International Offices:
London Toronto Melbourne

Copyright © 1973 by G. Airey, R. M. Bates, I. A. R. Price
Library of Congress Catalog Card Number 71-39887
ISBN 0 442 29951 6

The authors would like to thank Antony Atha for his help and advice.

All rights reserved. No part of this work covered by the copyrights hereon may be reproduced or used in any form or by any means — graphic, electronic, or mechanical, including photocopying, recording, taping, or information storage and retrieval systems — without permission of the publishers.

Design and lay-out by Rod Josey
Printed and bound in Spain
by Mateu Cromo Artes Gráficas, S.A.—Pinto (Madrid).

Published by Van Nostrand Reinhold Company, Inc., 450 West 33rd Street, New York, N.Y. 10001, and Van Nostrand Reinhold Company Ltd., 25–28 Buckingham Gate, London S.W.1.

Published simultaneously in Canada by Van Nostrand Reinhold Limited.
16 15 14 13 12 11 10 9 8 7 6 5 4 3 2 1

Contents

1	Introduction	7
2	Shape Development: A Modular System	9
3	The Principle of Folding	19
4	The Use of the Tube	33
5	Card Strips	43
6	Applied Decoration	55

Introduction

First we shall explain how to build a number of flat shapes, and then deal with making three-dimensional models by means of folds, slots, tubes and other constructional principles. The final chapter suggests various kinds of decoration and some less obvious developments such as printmaking.

One of the most rewarding activities for both children and adults is making all kinds of models and constructions. A large number of construction kits are sold every year covering a wide variety of materials such as wood, plastic, foil, metal and rubber, but however good they are, these sets do not often give much opportunity for creative self-expression. This is a pity, because most people have some kind of creative ability which can and ought to be developed. Designing and making something from one's own ideas can be very satisfying. The pleasure lies in doing something creative, and the educational and psychological benefits are also considerable.

Naturally certain guidelines are needed to give the individual a lead or springboard from which to develop his or her own ideas. The main aim of this book is to give such a lead by showing various simple methods of card and paper construction. We begin by introducing a Modular System, based on squares, triangles and circles, which we hope will prove a helpful starting point for anyone unsure of their imaginative and creative abilities. The designs based on this modular approach can be either simple or complex, and they can be decorated with a wide range of colours, patterns and textures.

Shape Development: A Modular System

A square piece of card or paper can be made to produce a number of different shapes. You can cut it into various sorts of triangles, divide it into rectangles, strips or even lines, and you can, of course, vary the size of the square. You can also do the same with circles, dividing them into halves, segments and so on.

The first step is to build up a large stock of these assorted shapes, and this will give you some practice in measurement and area. At first it is a good idea to limit yourself to black and white shapes, so that you can study the effect of counter-change, that is, white on black and black on white. Later on you can use coloured, toned and transparent papers for more sophisticated effects. A flannelgraph, using black and white felt shapes, could also be useful.

10

Having sorted out measurement, scale and proportion, the next stage is to arrange the shapes into various forms. Although initially this system may seem somewhat rigid and controlled, you will soon realize that the possibilities are endless. The illustrations give some indication of the range of ideas that can be developed within this framework.

Here is the growth of a flower, from its simple beginning to a complex design.

This town scene shows a similar approach. Additional features such as windows and doors made of black card are superimposed on the white shapes.

16

The principle of 'simple to complex' is clearly shown in this horse series.

These are examples of work by young children at a pre-school play group.

When the shapes have been arranged in a satisfactory design, they can be glued or pasted on to a background of card or paper and decorated in a variety of ways.

The Principle of Folding

In this chapter the flat shape is developed, in some cases with a mirror image, by folding it in a variety of ways so that it becomes a three-dimensional object. You will see that many designs have developed from the ideas suggested by the modular system.

When folding, a bone folder or similar implement can be used to score the card or paper in order to obtain a sharp crease. A ruler or piece of wood will be of great help with the straight lines, and where pieces of paper need to be curved they can be pulled over the edge of a board or table, or 'combed' with a ruler. Here are some examples of fold variations.

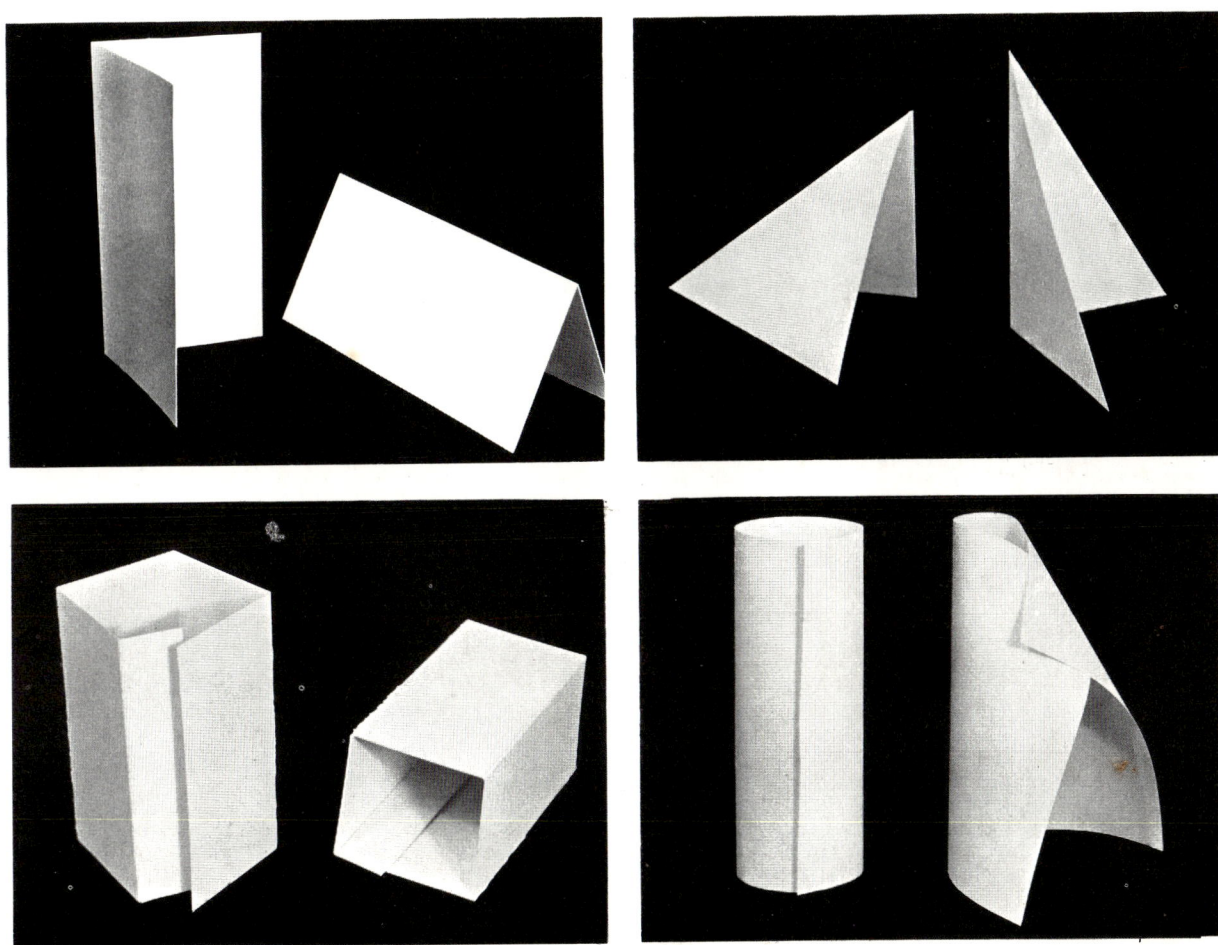

Most folded shapes will stand upright by themselves, but occasionally some form of support may be necessary, especially if the model is in a room with an excessive draught. There are several ways of doing this.

A piece of card can be glued to the back of the model, or it can be glued to a base. Another method is to glue together several shapes which would not stand up on their own.

Sometimes a piece of card which has been folded and glued needs an extra strip of card inserted at the back, or inside, to act as a form of brace and help the model keep its shape. It can be used either to keep the pieces apart or to bring them closer together.

A useful tip is to hold adjoining pieces together during the course of construction with paper clips, clothes pegs or elastic bands, until the glue is firmly set.

Here you see how easy it is to build up the figure of a horse or other animal. Start with the legs, body and neck, then add the head and tail.

22

Now we have taken the horse a stage further. The head, legs and body have been tapered a little, and additional features such as ears and tail have been glued on to the main structure.

The model can also be refined further by cutting curved shapes and other details to make the horse more realistic.

These two schoolchildren, aged eight and ten, are engaged in measuring, cutting and folding their individual animals.

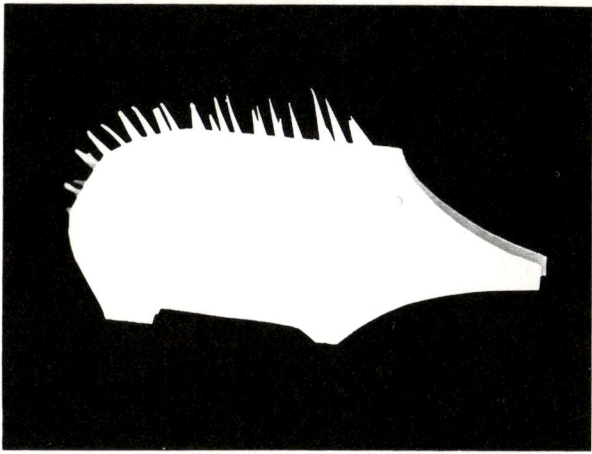

This series of birds and animals shows the life-like qualities that can be achieved by imaginative scissor-work.

Simple figures can be started in various ways, as shown here.

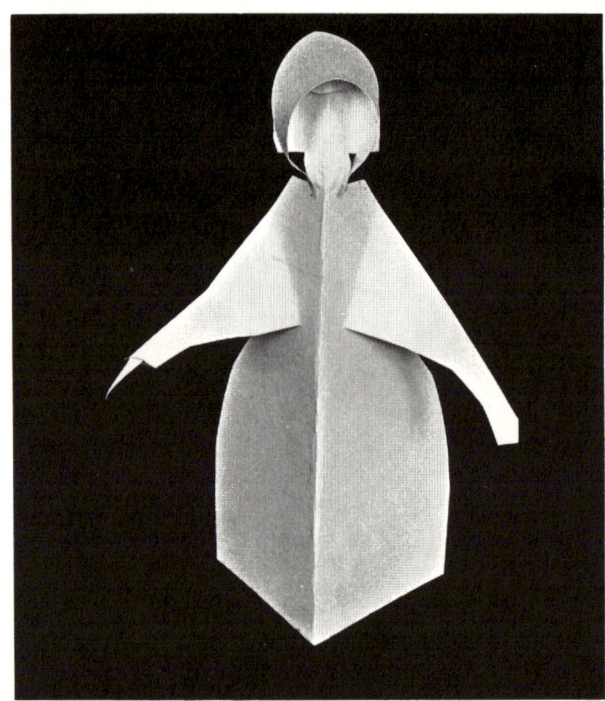

This group of conifers has been cut into in different ways. The pair in the centre were folded and their doubled edges cut simultaneously, giving the mirror image referred to earlier. In contrast, the edges of the trees on either side were cut separately.

The single conifer has had offcuts of card glued on to the main triangular shape to form the branches.

The principle of joining several pieces of folded card so that the whole unit stands up more easily is illustrated by the larger tuft of reed grass.

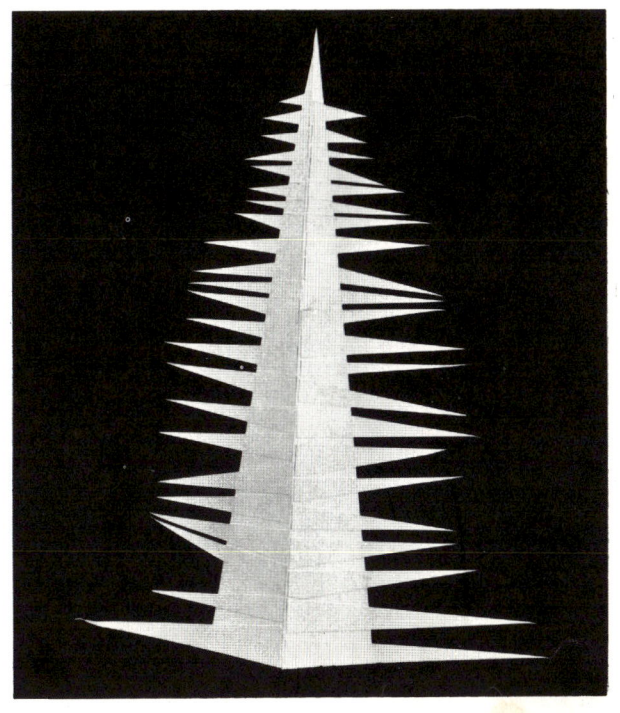

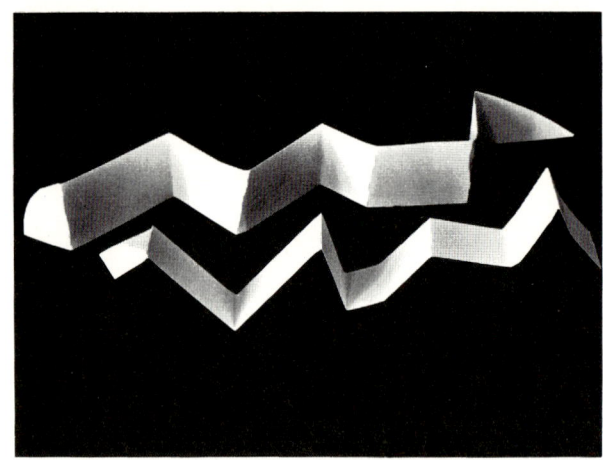

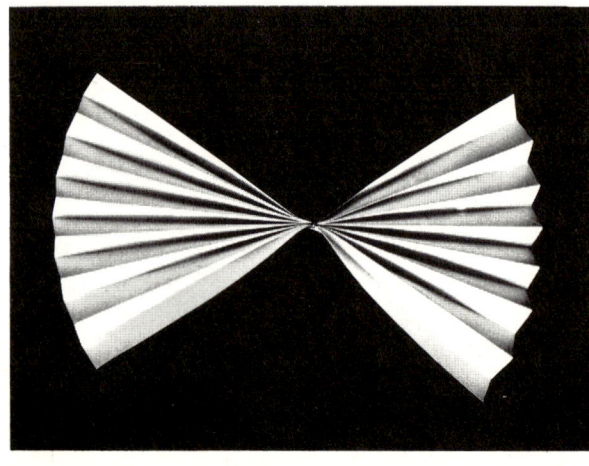

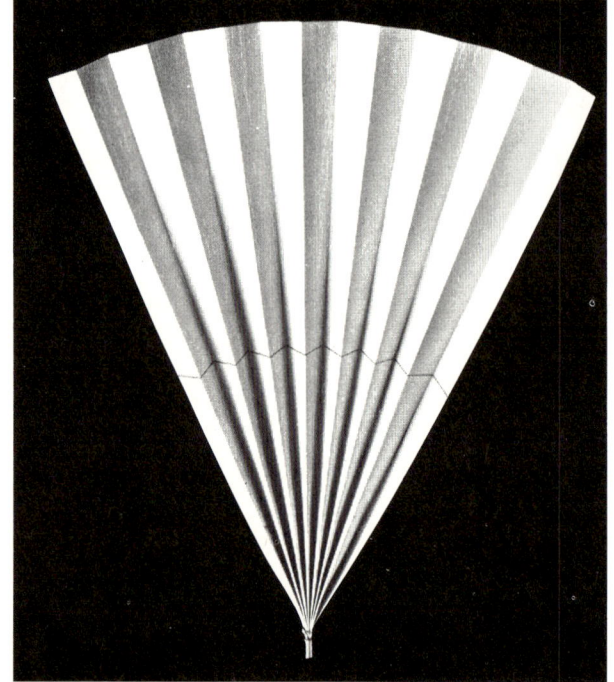

Opposite are some pieces of card that have been multi-folded. The strips have a snake or caterpillar-like quality, while the larger piece suggests a simple but effective group of buildings.

Another idea is to use a piece of stiff paper divided into equal sections and then scored and folded. We show two ways in which it can be developed.

This is a different type of folding. It uses two, three or more 'straight' folds, and it is ideal for building mechanical models such as lorries, tractors and aeroplanes.

On the following page we show the various stages in building a tractor. As you will see, we have used struts to help strengthen the body and support the mudguards.

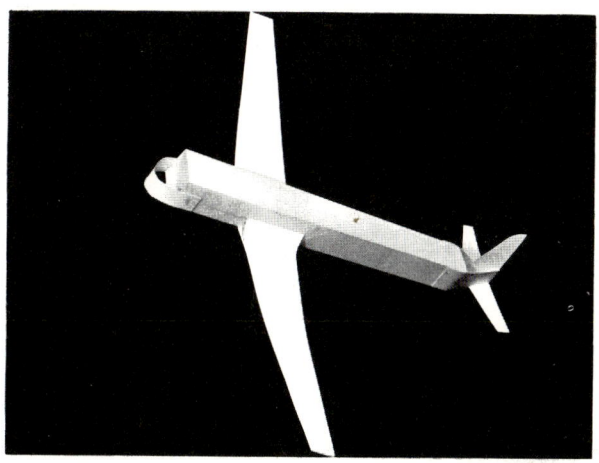

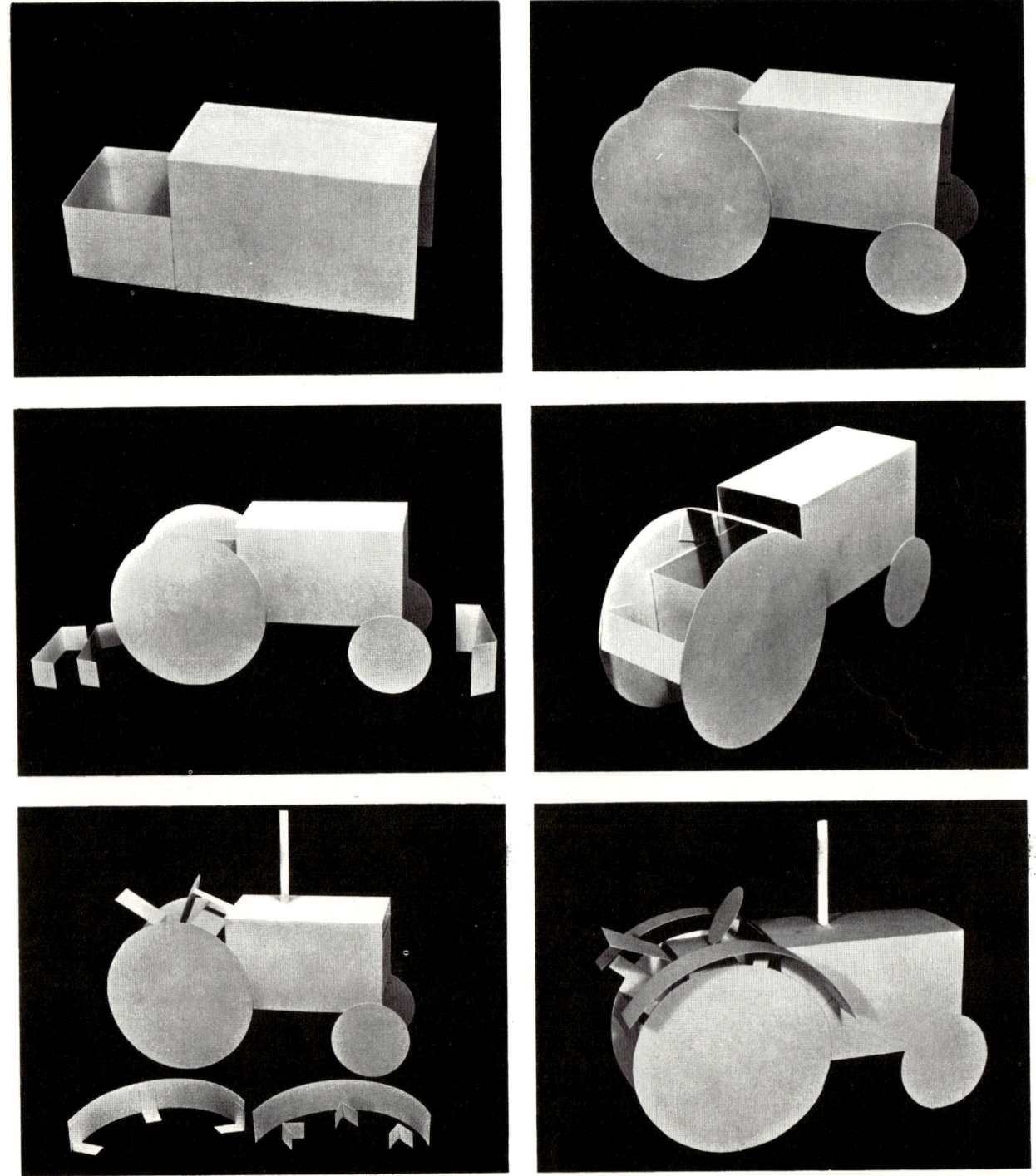

30

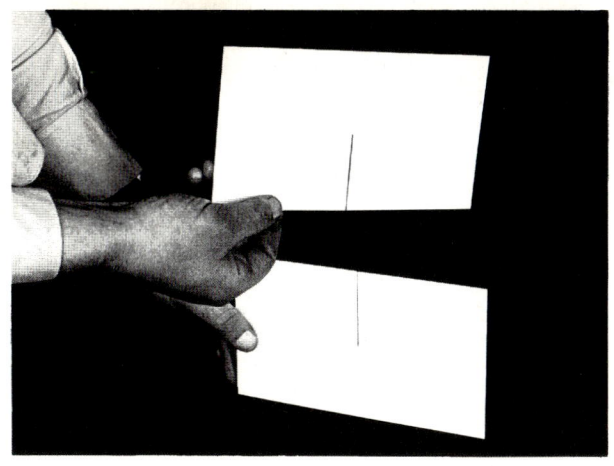
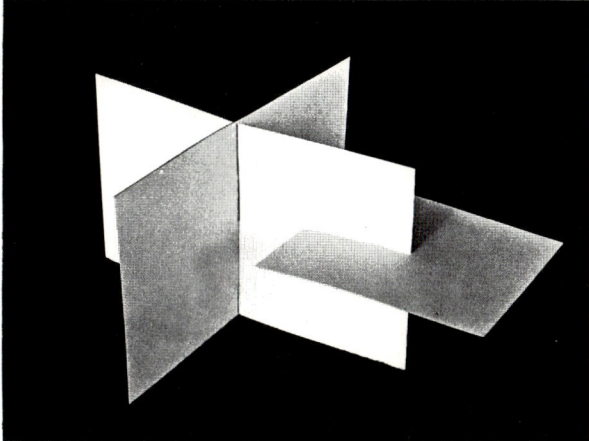

Introducing Slotted Card

The technique of folding can be further extended if we link up with the principle of slotting. You need two pieces of card: one is cut or slit halfway up from the bottom, and the other halfway down from the top. The two pieces are then slotted together to form a three-dimensional unit, and as the slots can be inserted vertically, horizontally or diagonally, the possibilities are endless. (If thick card is used, it is advisable to make the slots the same width as the card thickness, otherwise the pieces may buckle, tear or crack when they are put together.)

The abstract construction here was made from two rectangular pieces of card slotted together, which were then cut into and the strips bent in various directions. It could be either a free-standing unit or a mobile, and variations can be introduced by cutting into the card and adding extra decorative pieces. If you are making a mobile, glue the joints to prevent the unit from falling to pieces.

Folding and slotting is an ideal technique for making naturalistic forms such as animals, birds and trees. Here the lion's mane, which has been slotted on, is shown before being cut in a decorative way, and the other illustrations show a variety of animals.

One of the advantages of this principle is that the pieces can be made individually, in a confined space, before they are assembled. They can also be taken apart easily (unless they have been glued) and stored in a drawer or on a shelf.

The Use of the Tube

So far we have been looking at models made from folding and slotting paper and card, used either as separate techniques or in combination with each other. Except in a few cases where it was possible to introduce curved shapes, many of the models have had a 'flat surface look'. We can change this by the use of cylinders, which bring into play the attractive qualities of rounded forms and often present a pleasant three-dimensional appearance.

Although you can use ready-made tubes, these are usually limited in height and width, and it is much better to make your own. The best material to use is stiff paper, and you will find that paper clips and elastic bands are very useful in keeping the shape of the tube until the glue has set. Since tall, slender tubes are liable to fall over on occasions (unless several units are joined together), it is essential to have a good base. Two suitable bases are a flat piece of card, on to which the cylinder is glued, or a pill-box which can be filled with sand, plasticine or some other heavy material to weight the base. You can also make a number of cuts up the tube, spread out the flaps and glue them to the base.

If you need several tubes of the same size, they can easily be 'mass-produced' from the same jar or other cylindrical object.

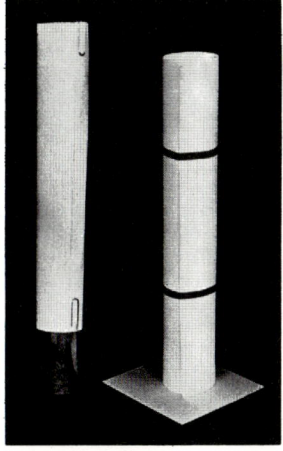
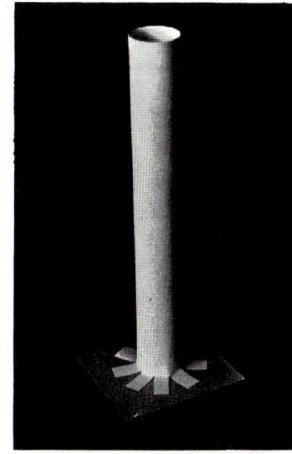
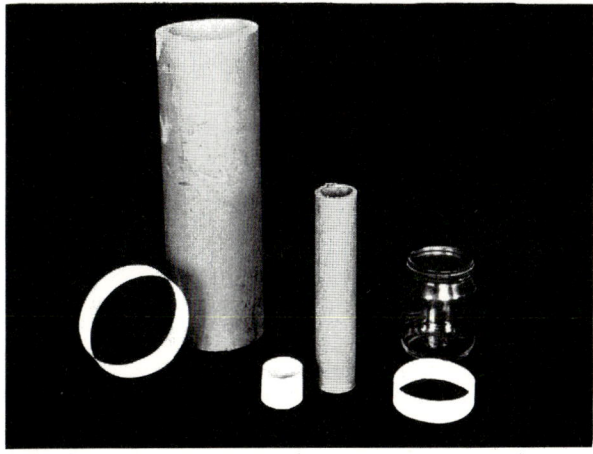

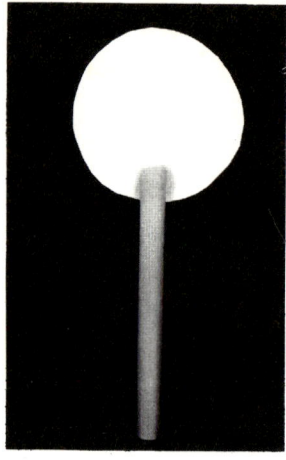 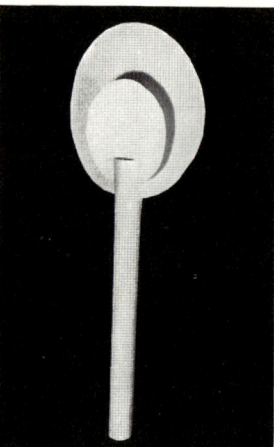 

A circular piece of card slotted to a tube might represent, to a young child, the basis of a tree, figure or flower.

The two superimposed discs of card give an interesting three-dimensional effect. The smaller one casts a shadow on the larger shape.

Interesting variations can be achieved by cutting into the slotted shapes.

 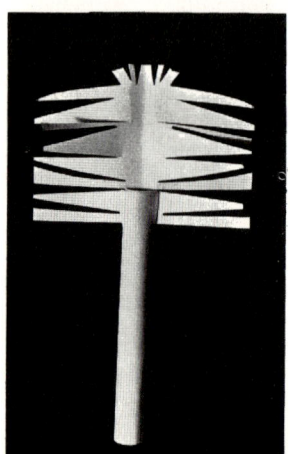

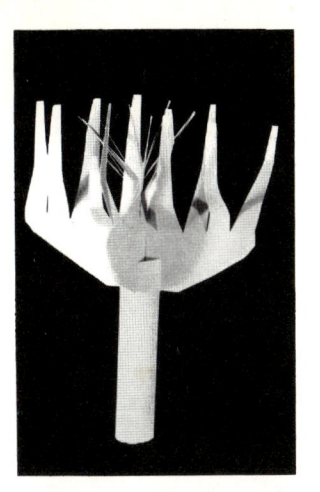

Two similar cut shapes are slotted on to the tube at right angles to give the impression of a flower head.

Offcuts from the previous models can be glued on to the basic shape of tube and disc in a decorative fashion.

Offcuts glued round the surface of a tube produce a tree-like effect. In this particular model two slotted triangles have been used to form the roots of the tree.

Another way of decorating the tube is by using pieces of card which are wrapped around it and glued together to form a single arm or branch. This principle could also be used to link several units together.

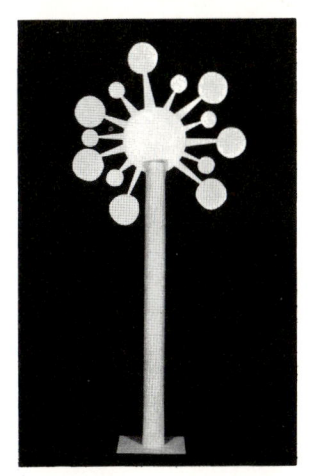

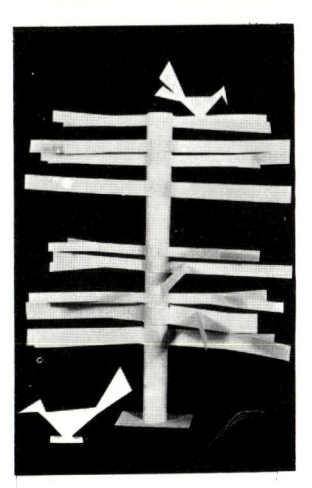

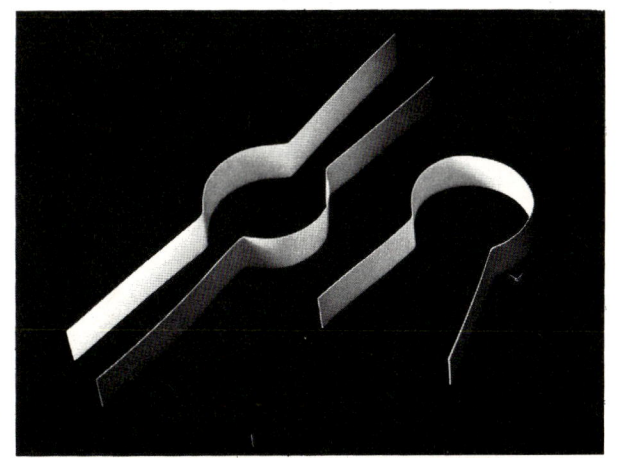

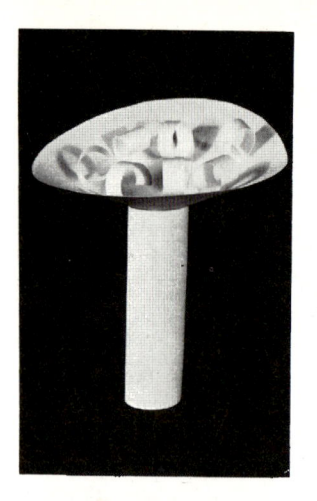

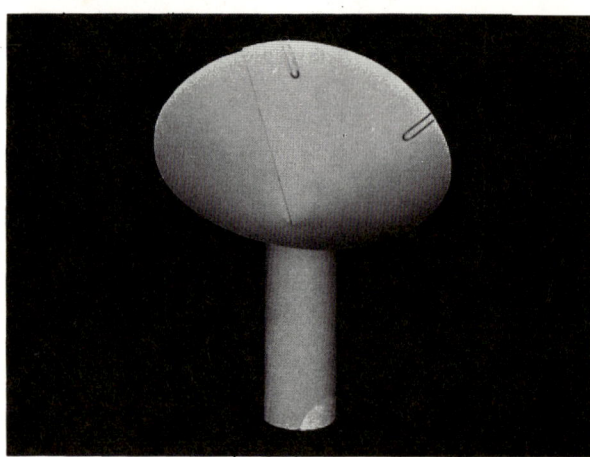

In addition to cylinders, cones can be very adaptable and lend themselves to attractive variations.

To make a simple cone, cut a radius slit in a circular disc of paper or thin card. Then pull the two edges into an overlap and trim and glue them. They can be held in place with paper clips until they are dry.

The cones are then ready for further developments. They can be decorated with several small cones, with curled strips of paper, and by cutting out and adding pieces.

If the tube has been made with plenty of overlap inside, cuts can be made with scissors from the top and the resulting shapes opened out. You can vary the effect by using tubes of different heights, or by combining two together.

38

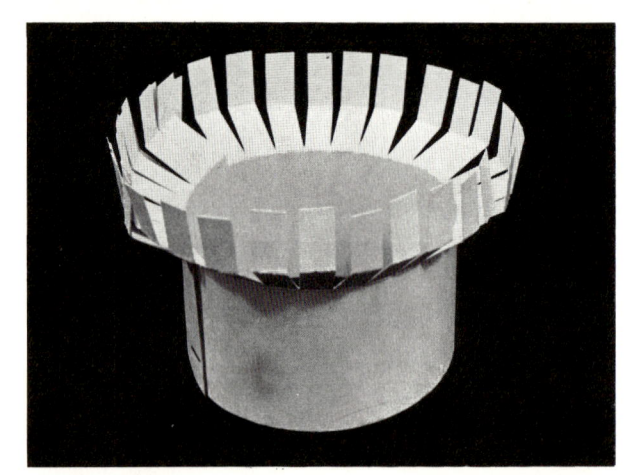

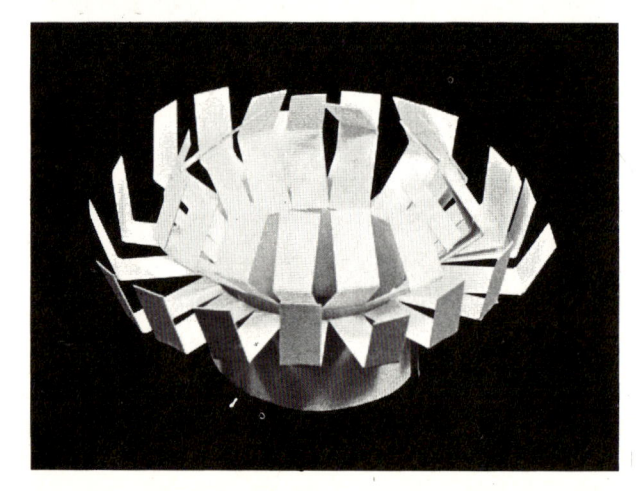

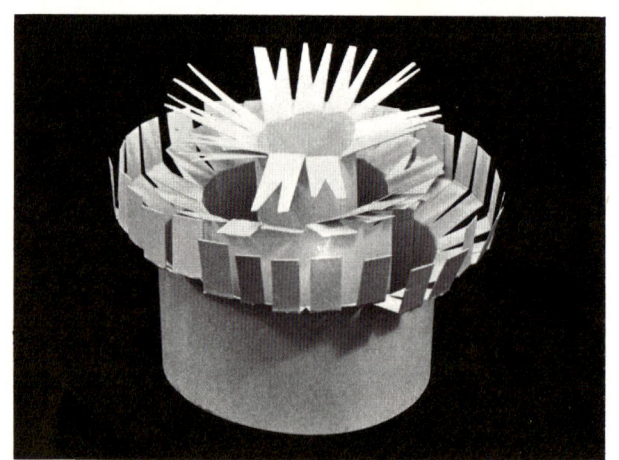

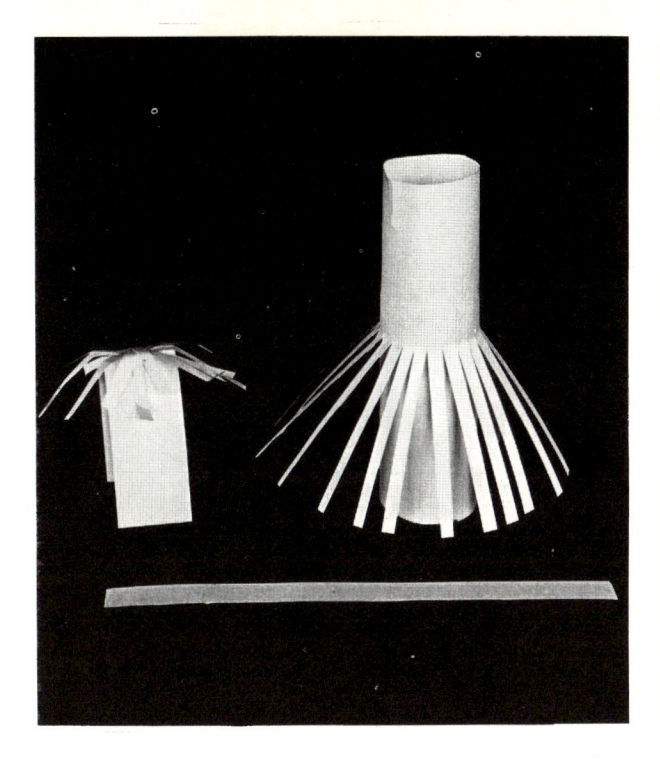

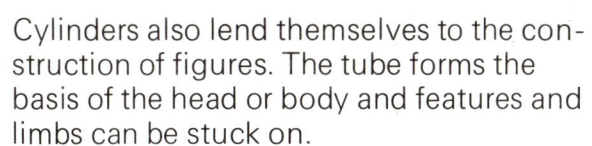

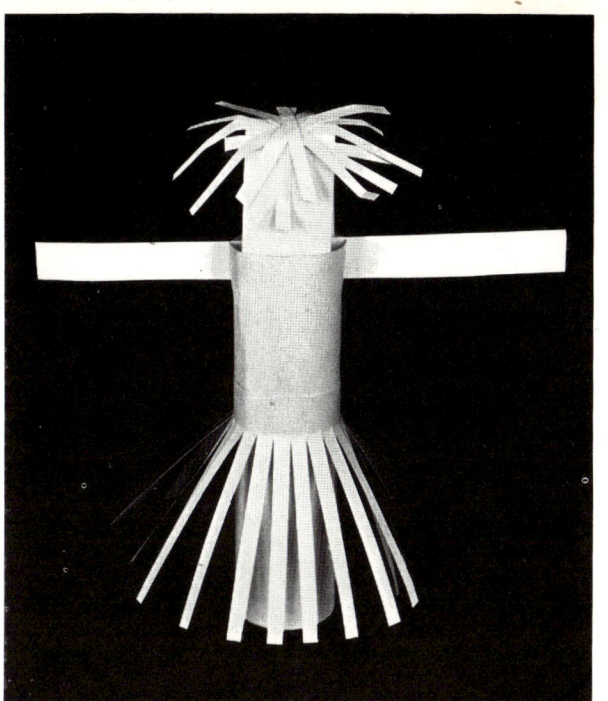

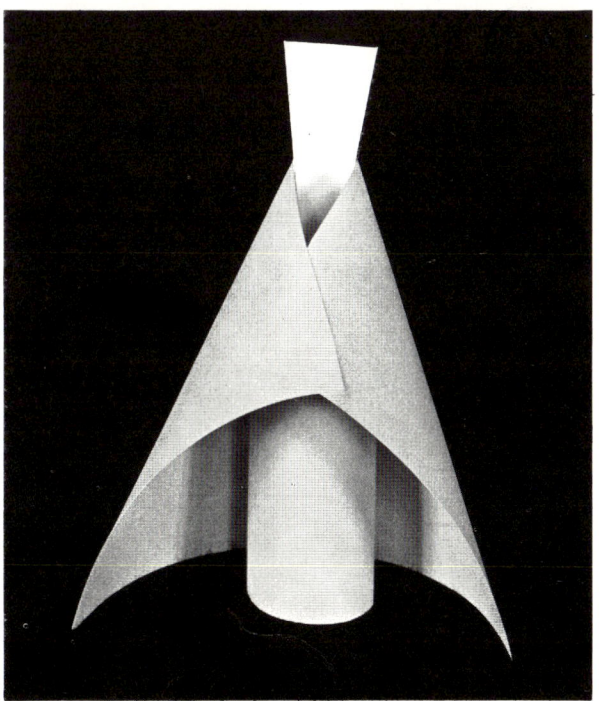

Cylinders also lend themselves to the construction of figures. The tube forms the basis of the head or body and features and limbs can be stuck on.

39

40

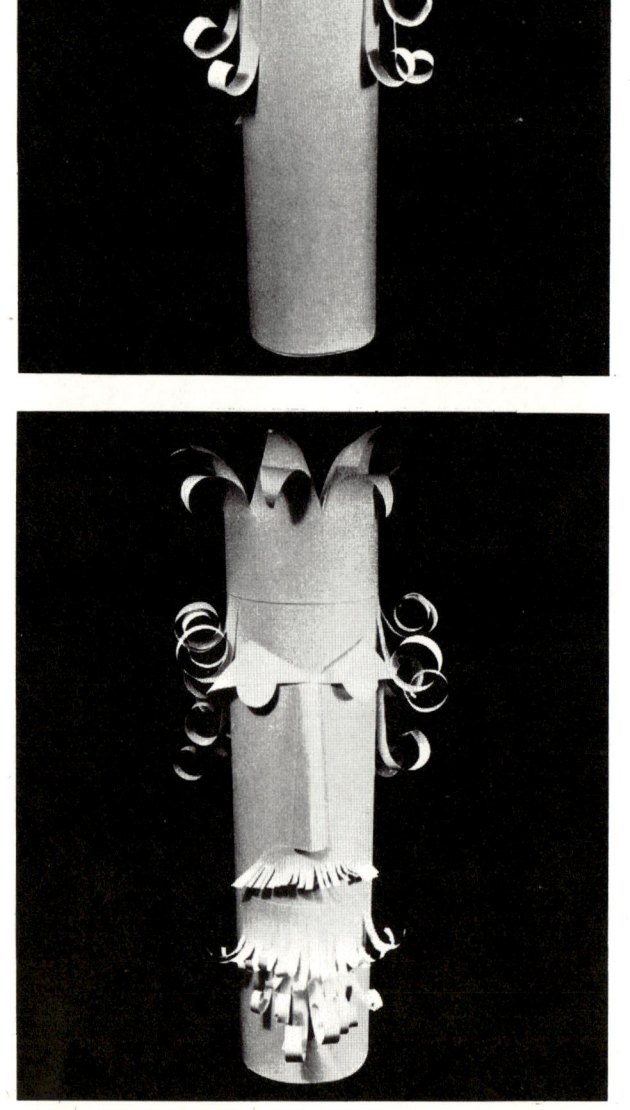

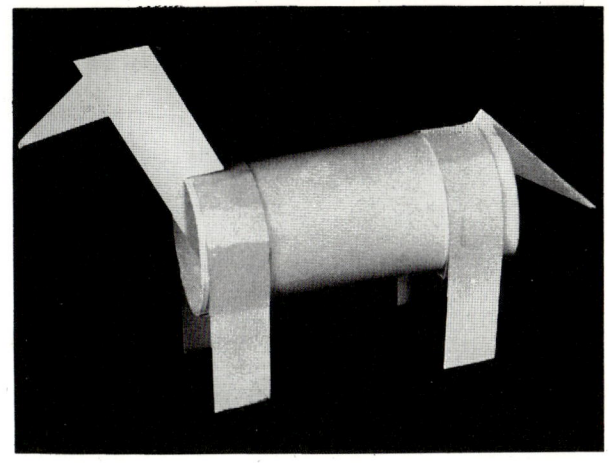

Animals and insects sometimes look more natural with a rounded body instead of the relatively flat surface which you get with folded or slotted models. The legs can be made of stiff card and glued over the top of the body. The llama's coat is built up in a similar way from strips of paper.

A simple system of articulation can be made by joining segments together with strips of paper or cotton and string. The illustration of the beginning of an articulated model shows a set of legs which support the body underneath in a trestle fashion. Both these principles are useful when modelling caterpillars, insects and reptiles.

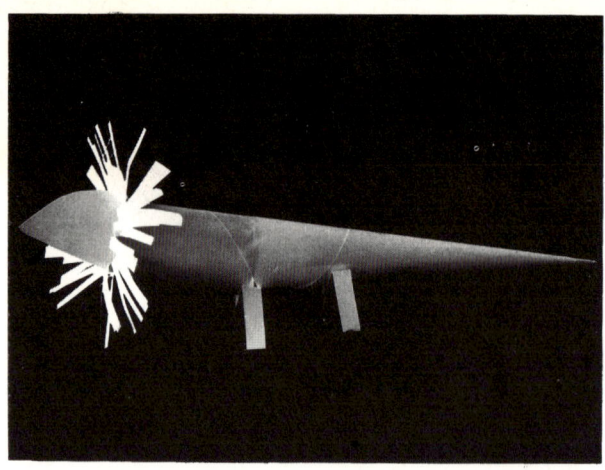

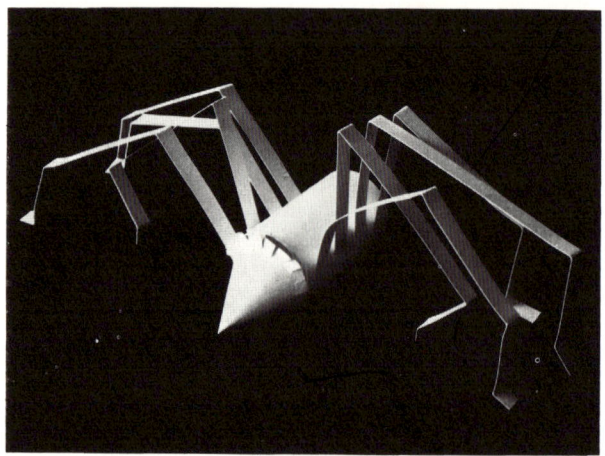

Models using different principles can be grouped together to form a scene. Here are two examples showing how attractive a group of plain white paper or card models can look against a plain background.

42

Card Strips

Now we move on to a technique that initially involves an 'open' framework or 'skeleton' type of construction which is built up from one or several basic shapes. Apart from the artistic and educational opportunities, card-strip projects give you a chance to use up all the offcuts of paper and card that accumulate in the junk-box. If you are short of material, try asking printers or book-binders, who are usually only too willing to dispose of the contents of their guillotine waste-bins.

The first step is to form a strip into one of the basic shapes. Glue one end and lap the other end over to complete the shape. You can keep this in place with a paper clip or clothes-peg until the glue has set. An excellent alternative, which will hold the pieces together even more quickly and effectively, is to use a stapling machine. Squares, triangles and circles can be formed, as well as other shapes.

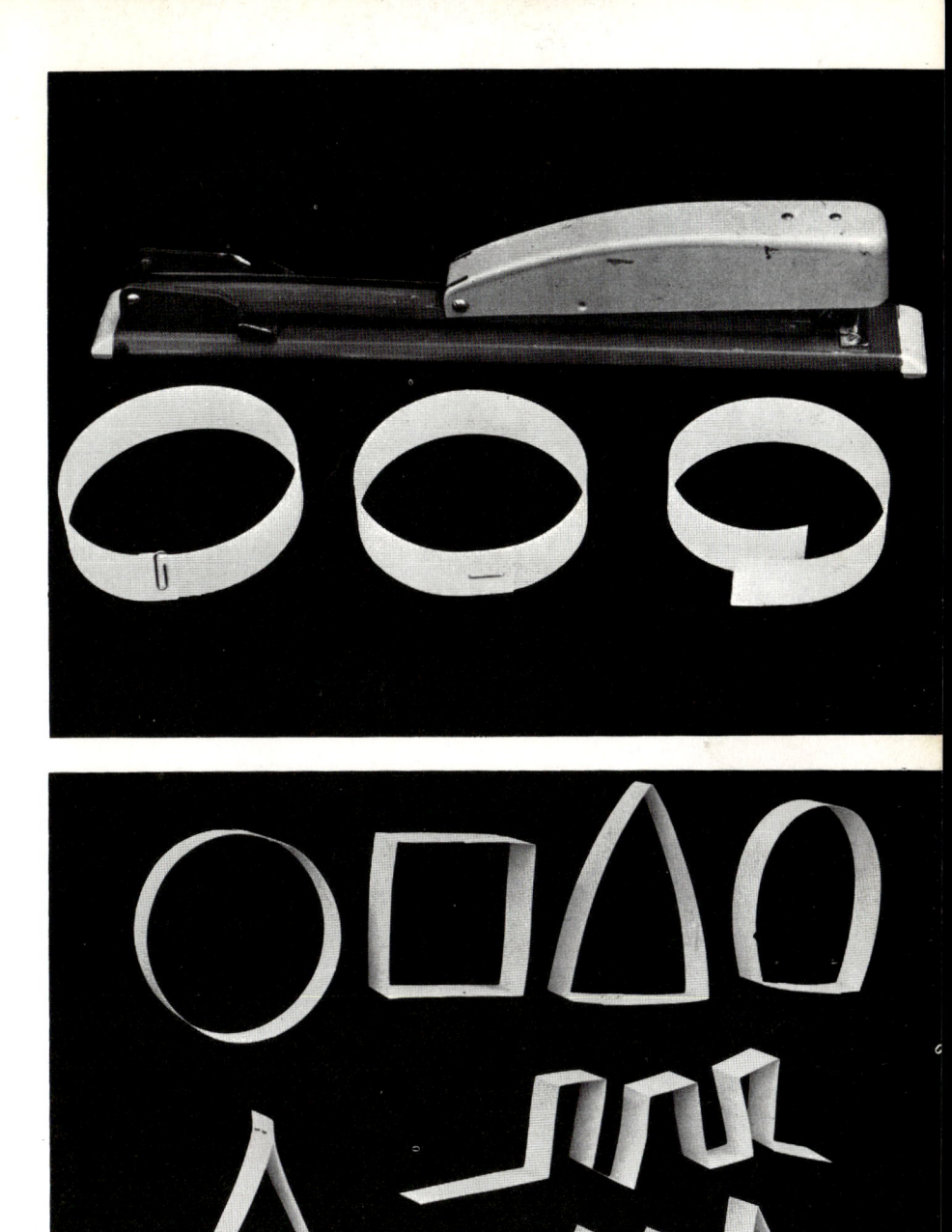

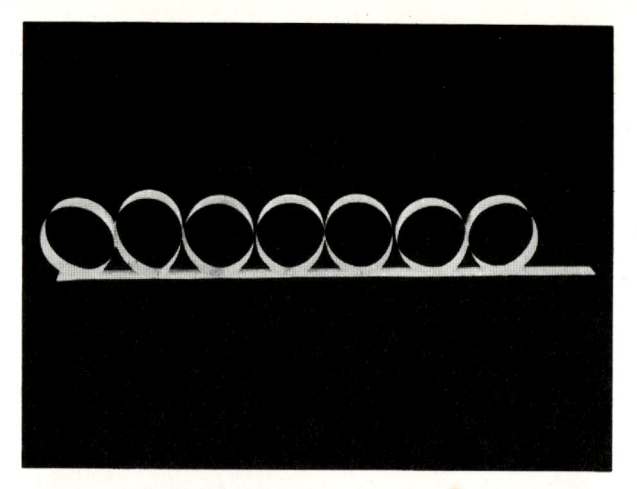

Sometimes a decorative unit can be made simply by allowing the pieces to assemble themselves spontaneously. The illustrations show how to build up a design from a row of identical circles and a long, straight strip of paper. The circles are glued to the strip which is then curved round to form a circle. The idea is extended by stretching a longer strip around the outside, and in the final motif pointed shapes have been added to the perimeter.

If you are doubtful about the final result, you can fix the construction with paper clips first, so that it is easy to make any necessary alterations. This can save time, expense and patience.

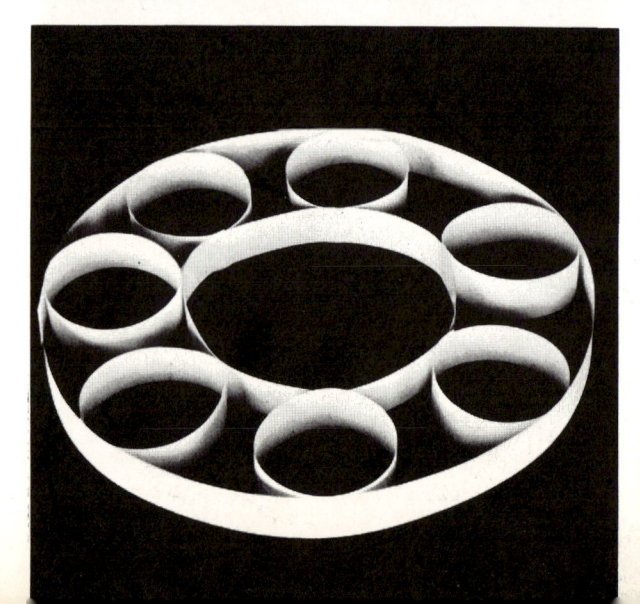

45

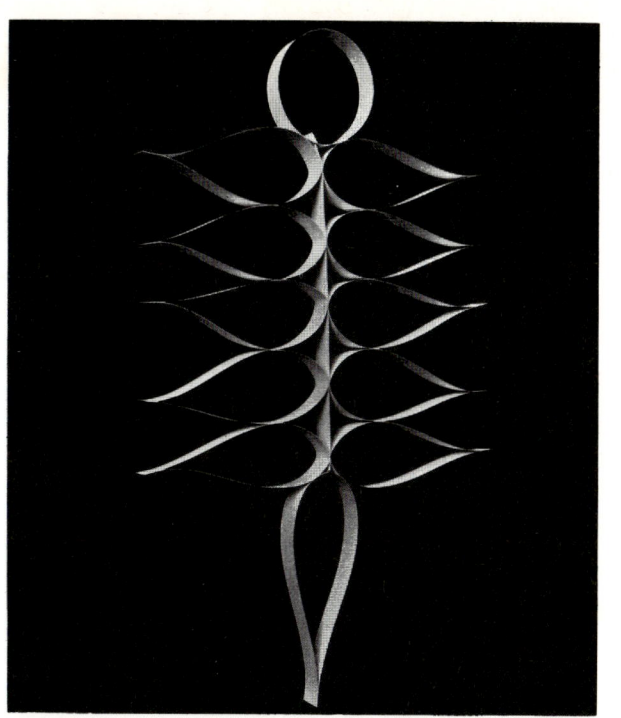

46

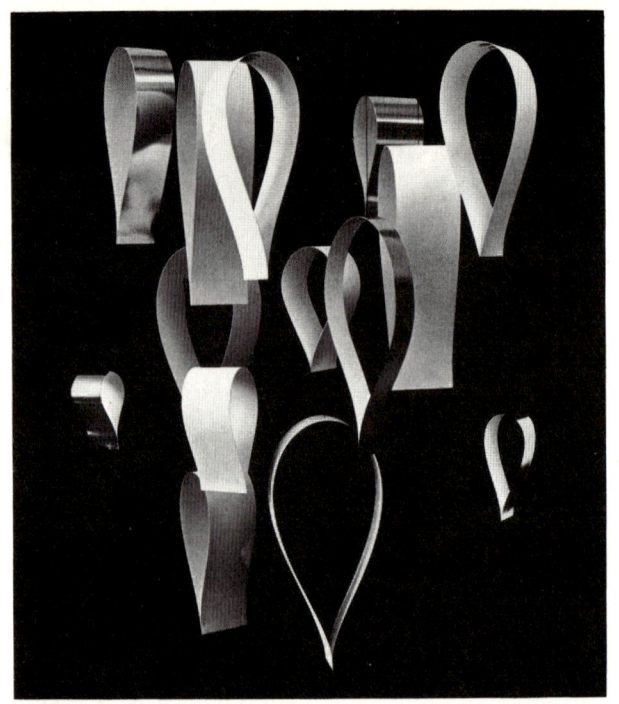

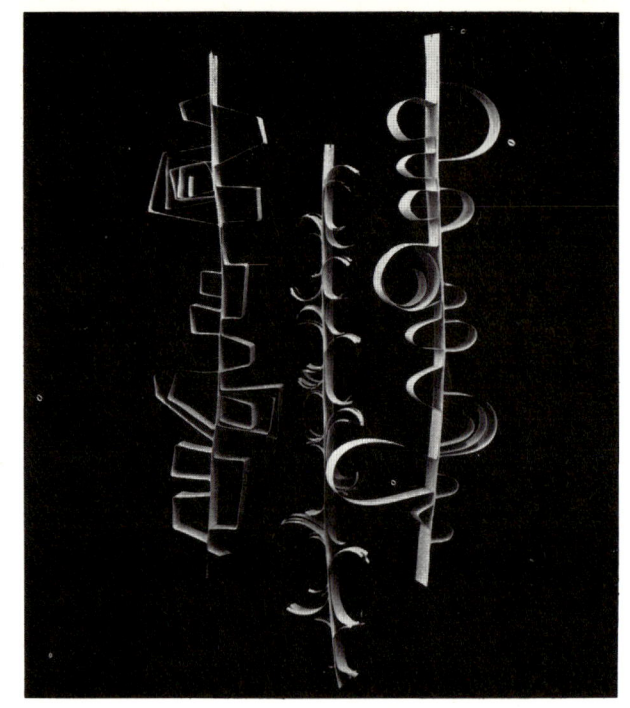

This particular process is perhaps most suitable for making mobiles. Hanging individual shapes by cotton or nylon thread from a ceiling, hoop, bar or old umbrella frame will create a situation where any slight movement of air will spin each piece in different directions, forming a constantly changing group. It can be very effective if you use strip shapes of silver or gold card, which have a sparkling quality which looks very attractive on festive occasions.

Sometimes a hanging shape can have another suspended inside it. The shapes can be either plain or decorated.

Plain strips of card can be embellished in a number of ways and then perhaps formed into a circular motif.

A number of basic shapes can be linked together and then joined end to end to make another variation of the circular unit. Other shapes, both large and small, can then be added to make a fairly complex construction. These figures can be adapted to a variety of uses such as mobiles, tree shapes, chandeliers and candelabra.

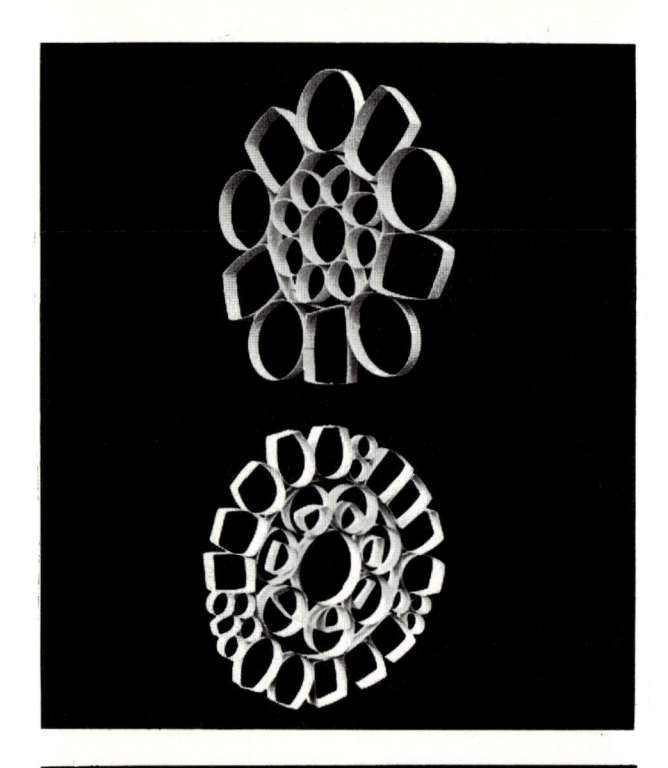

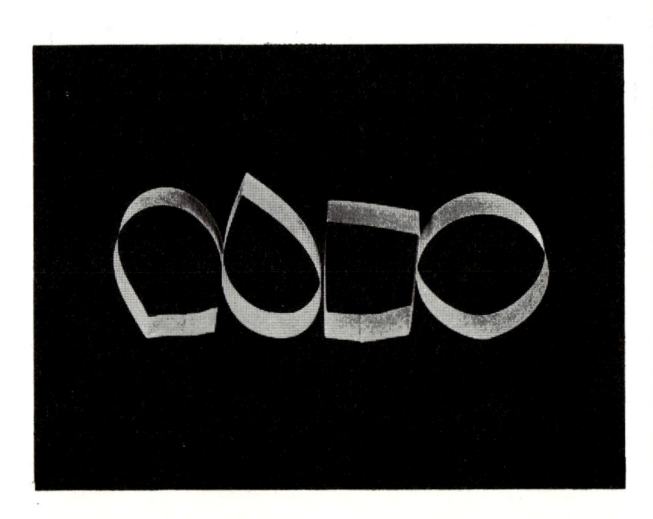

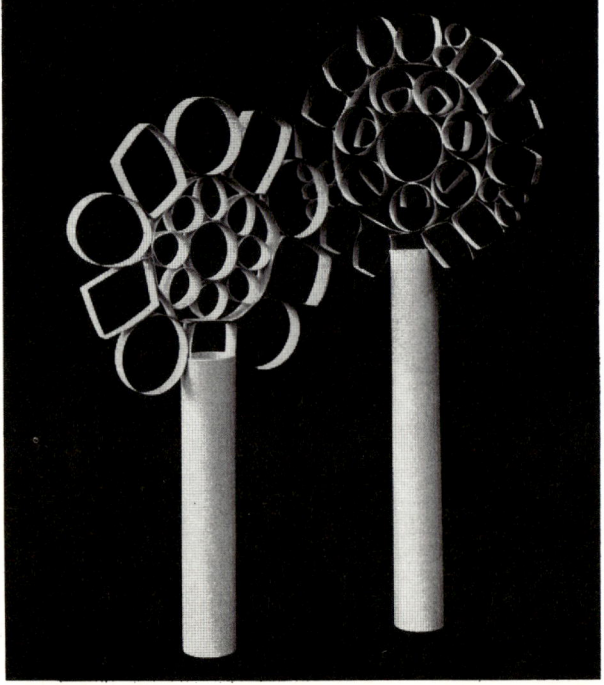

49

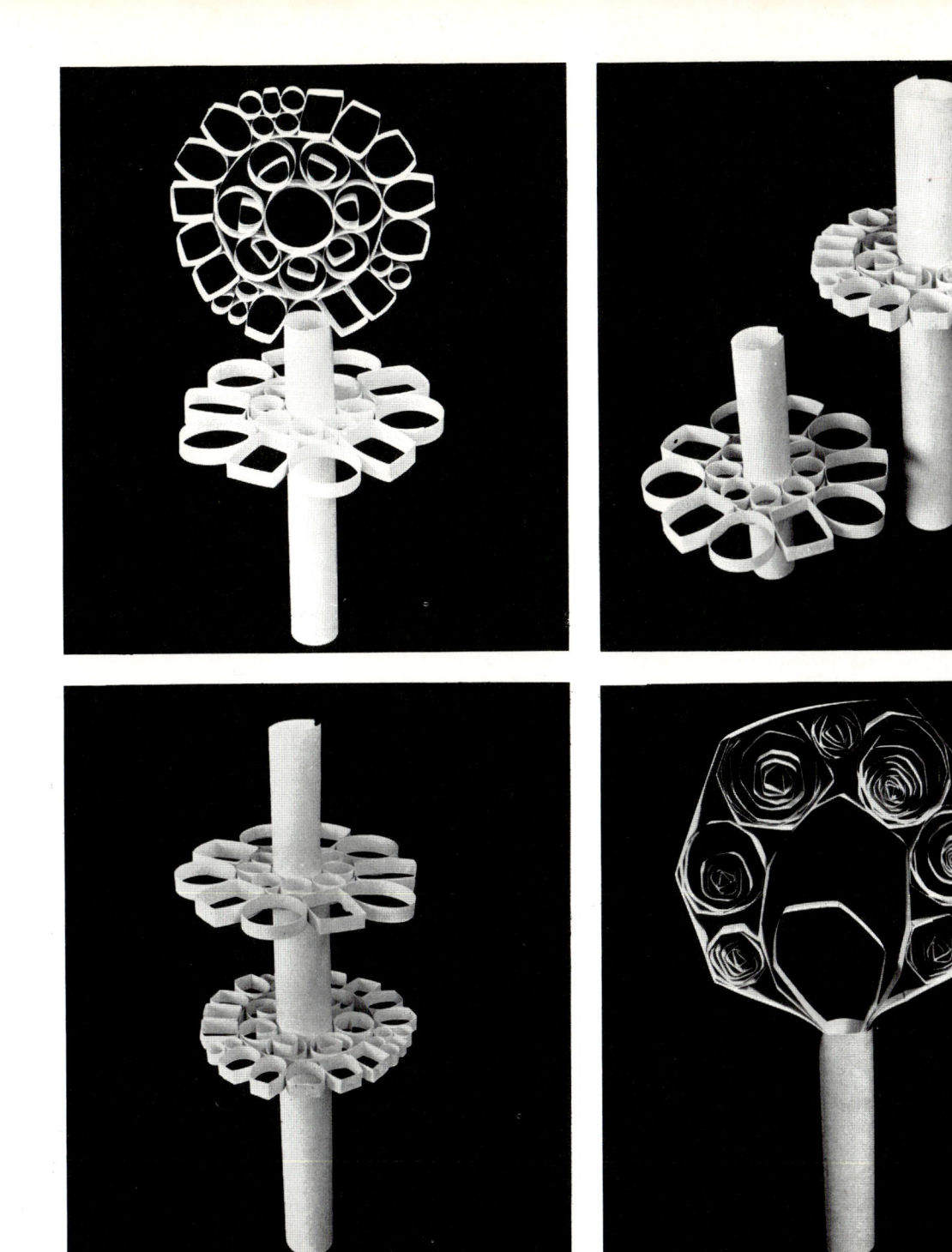

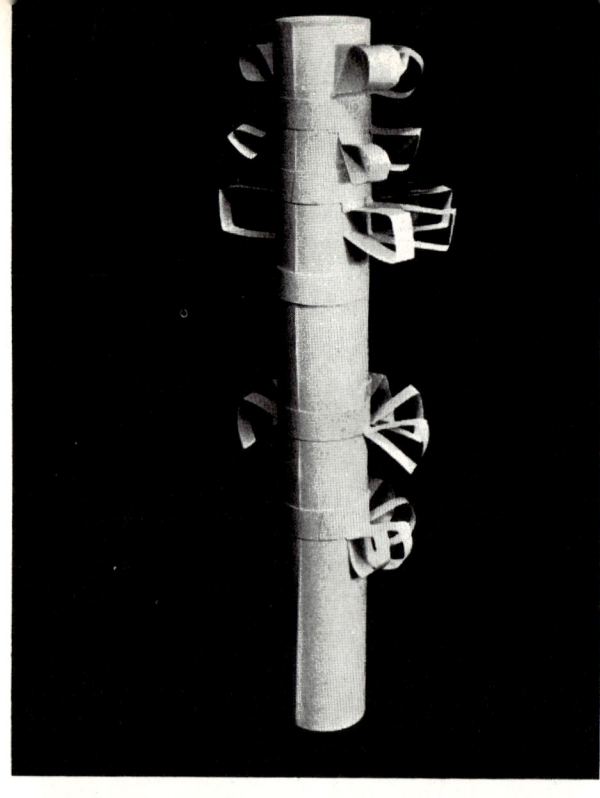

One idea for a tree shape is to use strip coils to fill in the main shapes, which are contained within the tube. It is not always necessary to glue every piece of card or paper together, as the natural spring tension of coiled or curved paper is often sufficient to hold a construction in place.

Here is an idea for using the tube as the principal means of support for the strips. First of all a piece of paper is wrapped fairly tightly around the cylinder. Then a number of strips are slipped through this 'collar' and bent or folded to form an interesting series of shapes. Naturally you can use as many collars as you like, and if several are wrapped around the tube, the permutations of design which you can achieve are considerably extended. As you will see from the illustrations, some strips are bent into curves and some are folded, while the grouping of these elements is also varied.

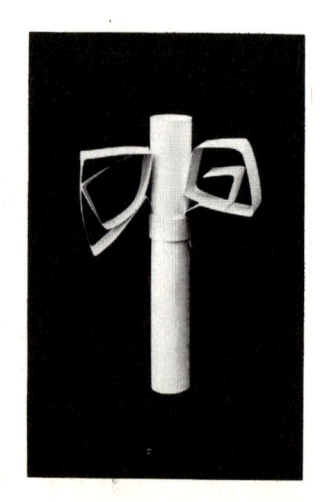

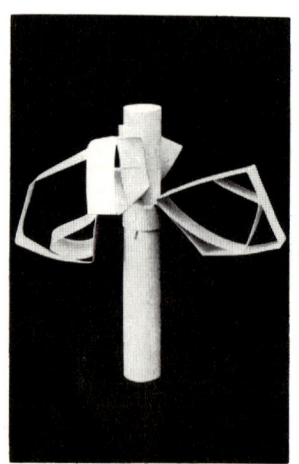

50

51

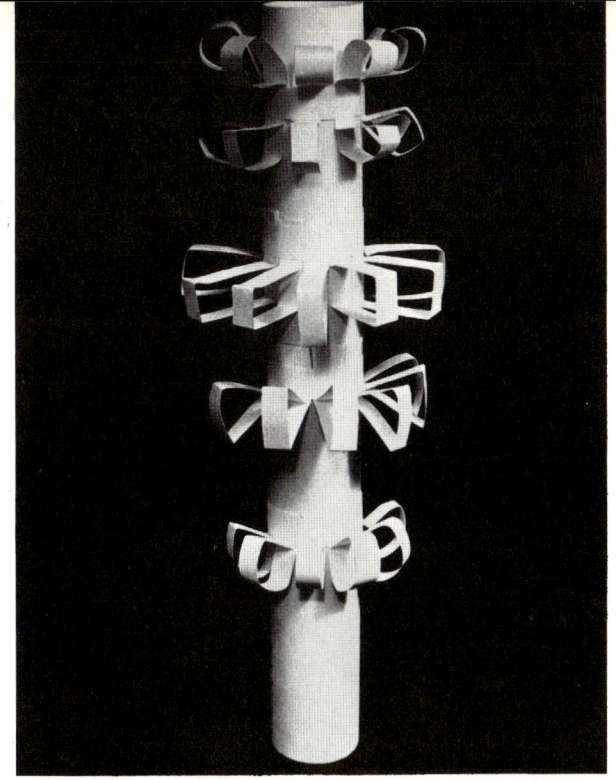

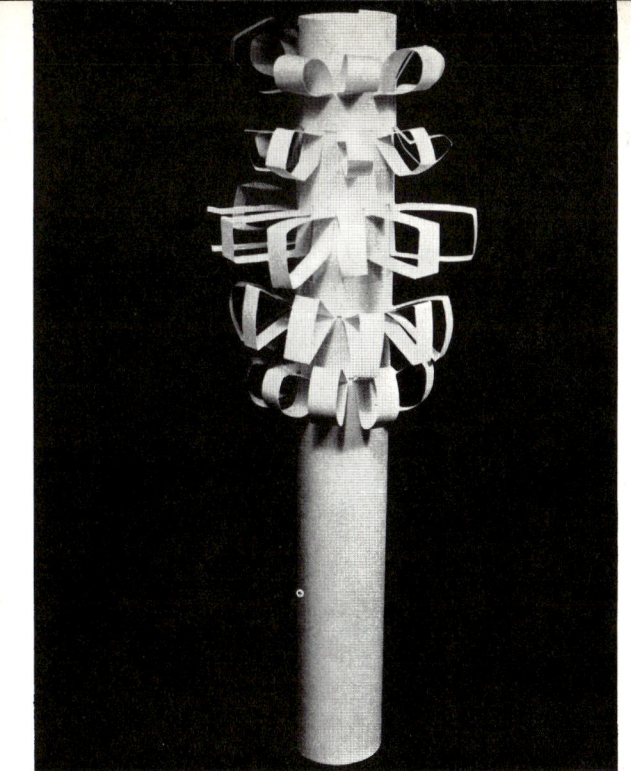

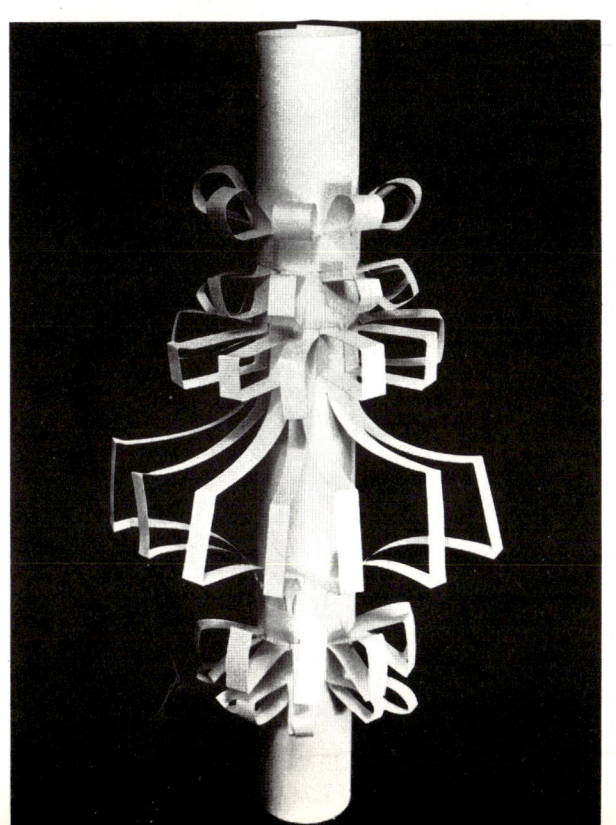

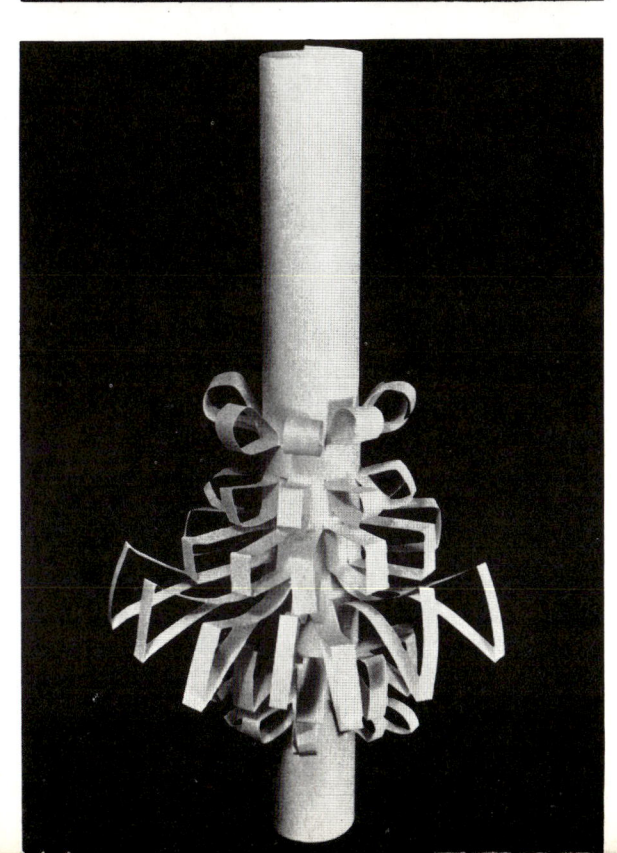

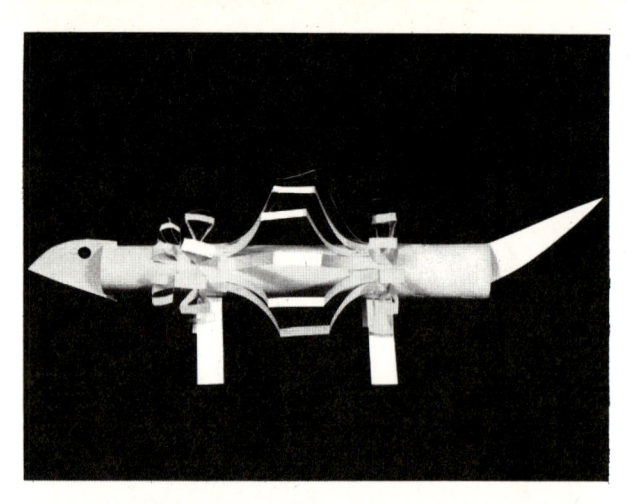

Adding strips to a basic shape such as a tube or a loop can change or enlarge its possibilities. Here we see various examples which have been constructed on this principle.

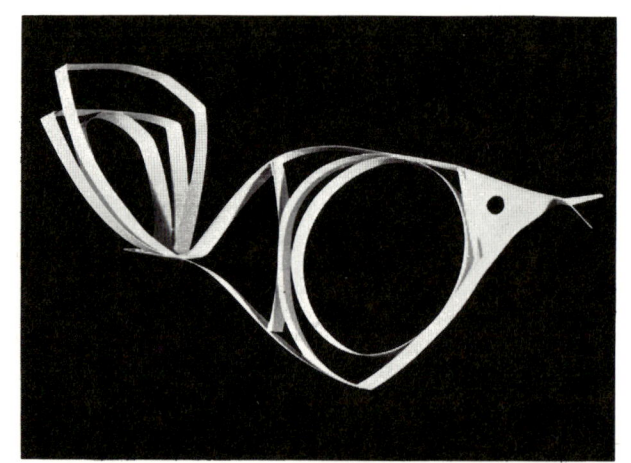

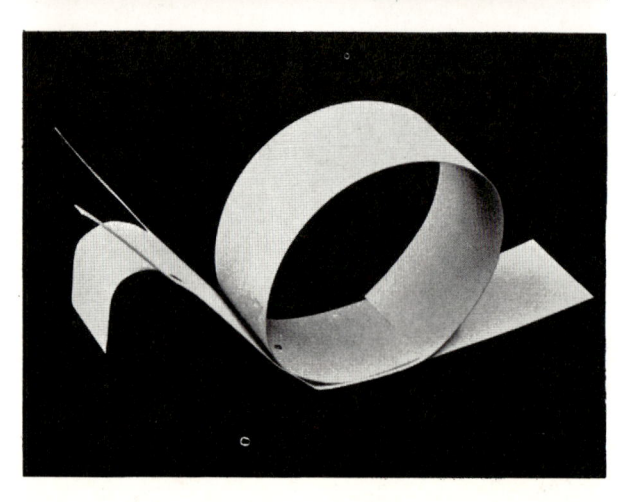

52

By using relatively simple 'framework' shapes, you can produce some very imaginative and effective birds, fishes and animals.

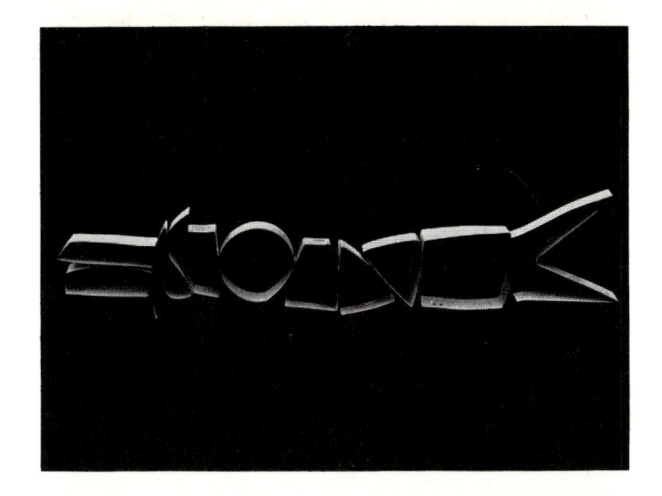

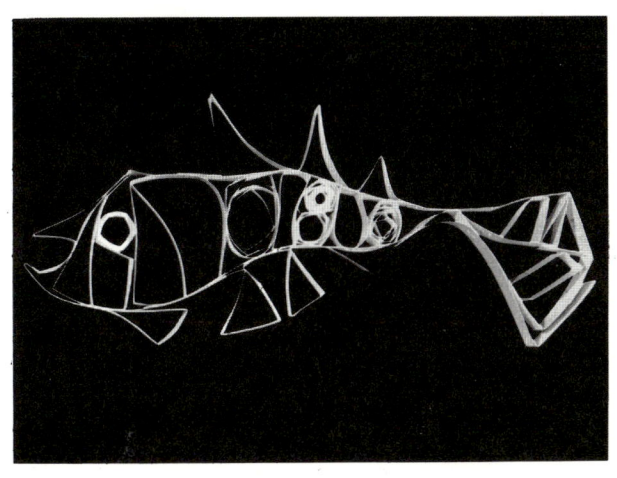

54

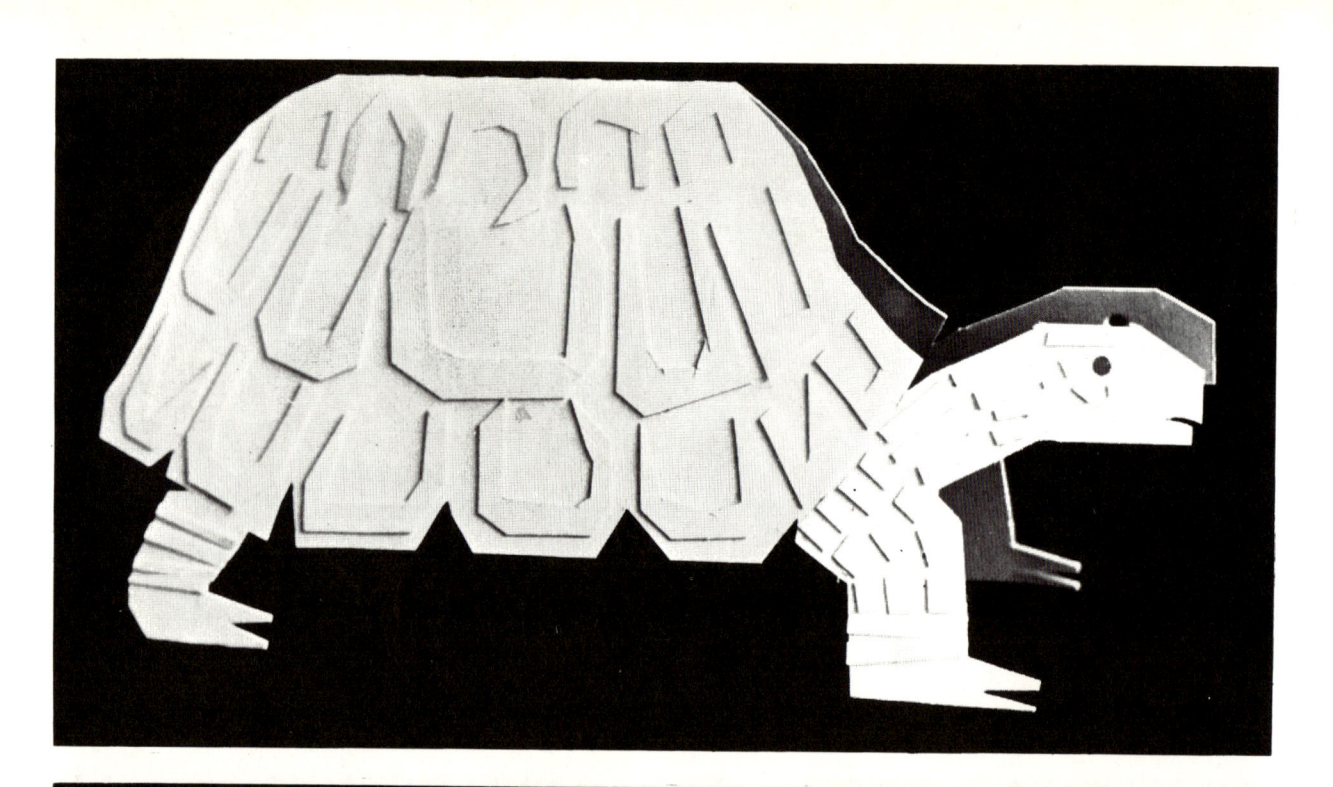

Applied Decoration

Relief Surface — Cut Paper, Card and Other Materials

We suggested earlier that some models look attractive enough if they are not coloured at all but left plain white or in their natural state. Decorative effects can be achieved by cutting into shapes, or by glueing on offcuts of card or paper. Creating relief surfaces is an area which offers many opportunities for exploring a rich variety of patterns and textures, and in which other materials such as straw, raffia, string and so on can be used to advantage. It should also encourage you to look carefully at natural textures, such as feathers, scales, fur and wool, as well as trying to make entirely imaginative patterns.

Relief decoration can be added to most flat and some curved forms. The fish on the right uses flat pieces of card and coiled strips, and the animals on the following pages use cut or torn paper and card pieces to create fairly flat, low-relief effects.

Bear in mind that this method should give you the chance to explore other areas. For example, if a thin piece of paper is placed over a relief-surface design, then 'rubbed' with wax or oil crayons, or rolled with a printing roller charged with a thin film of printing ink (as for a brass-rubbing), a number of impressions or prints can be taken.

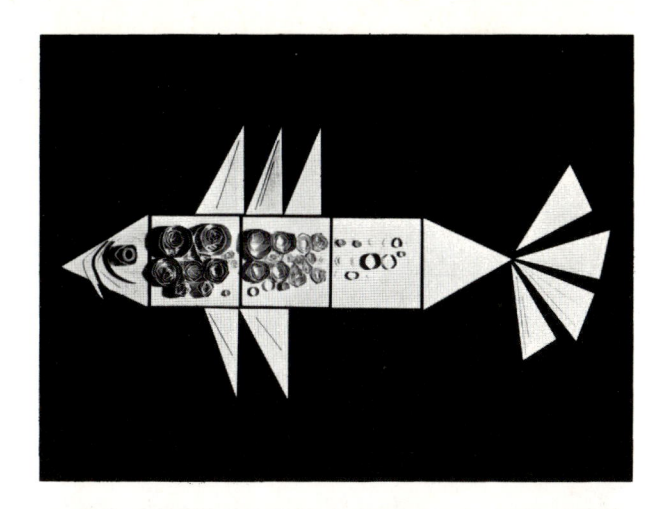

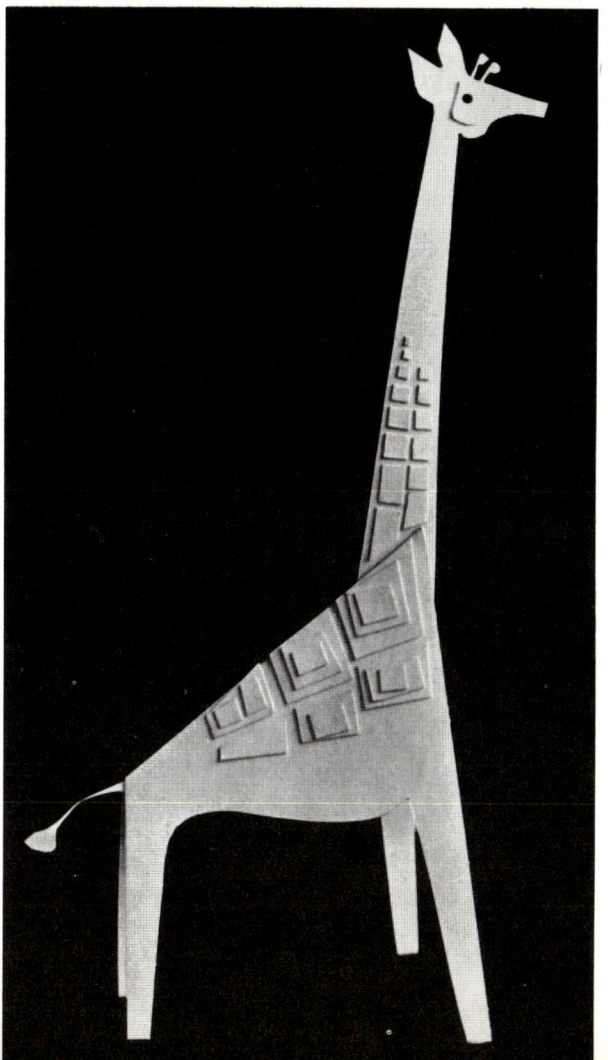

56

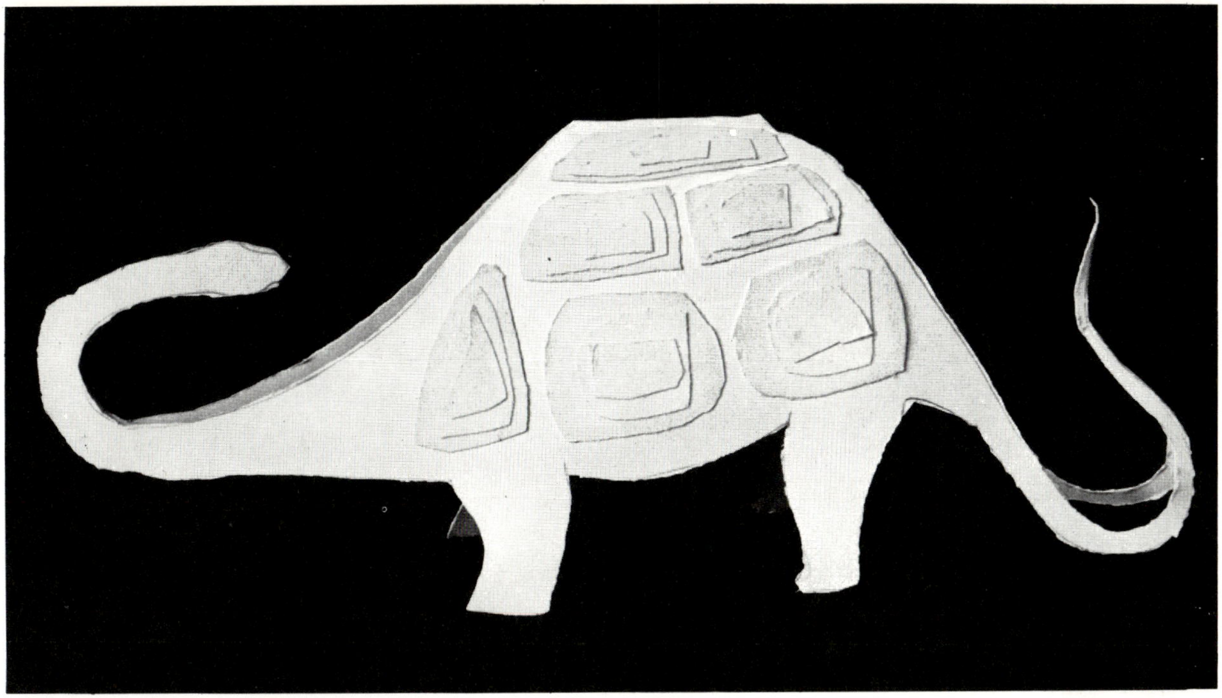

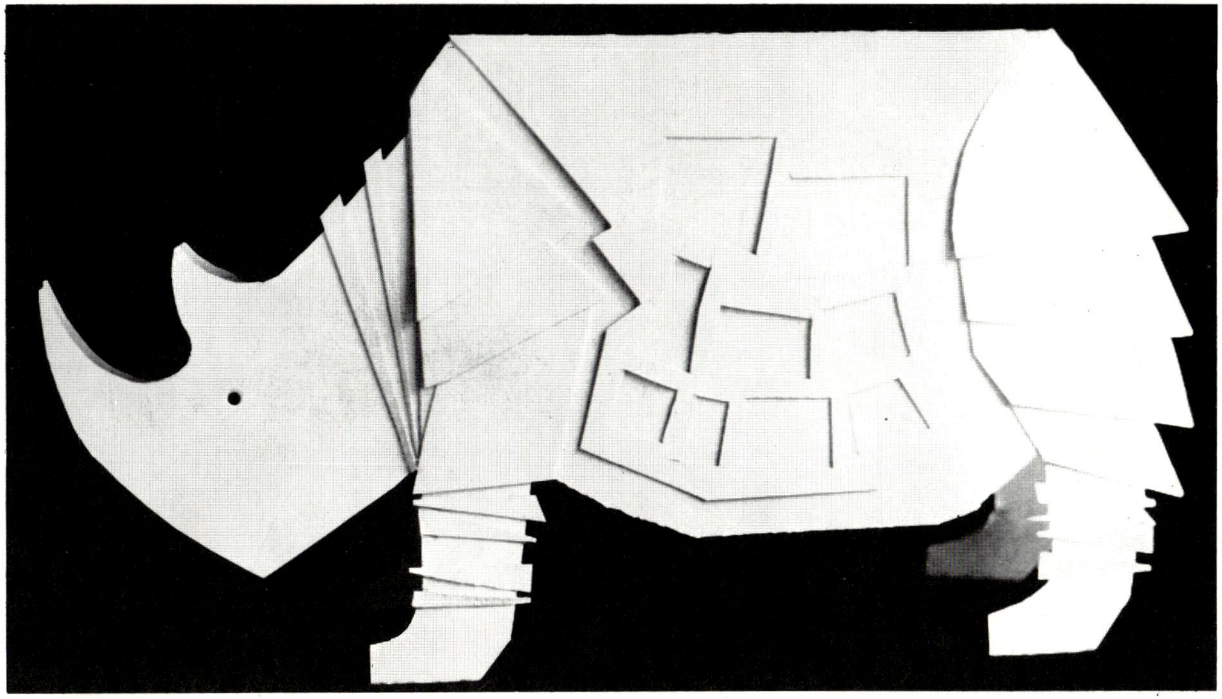

58

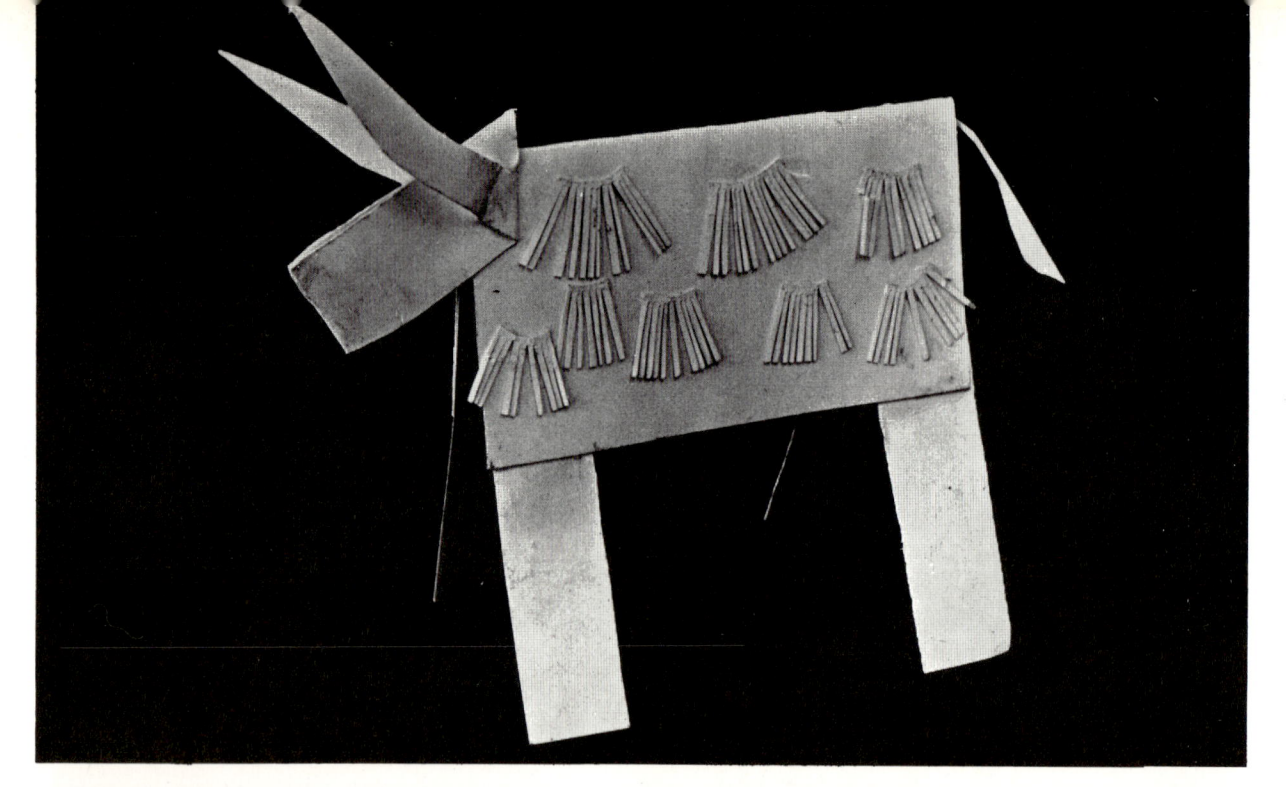

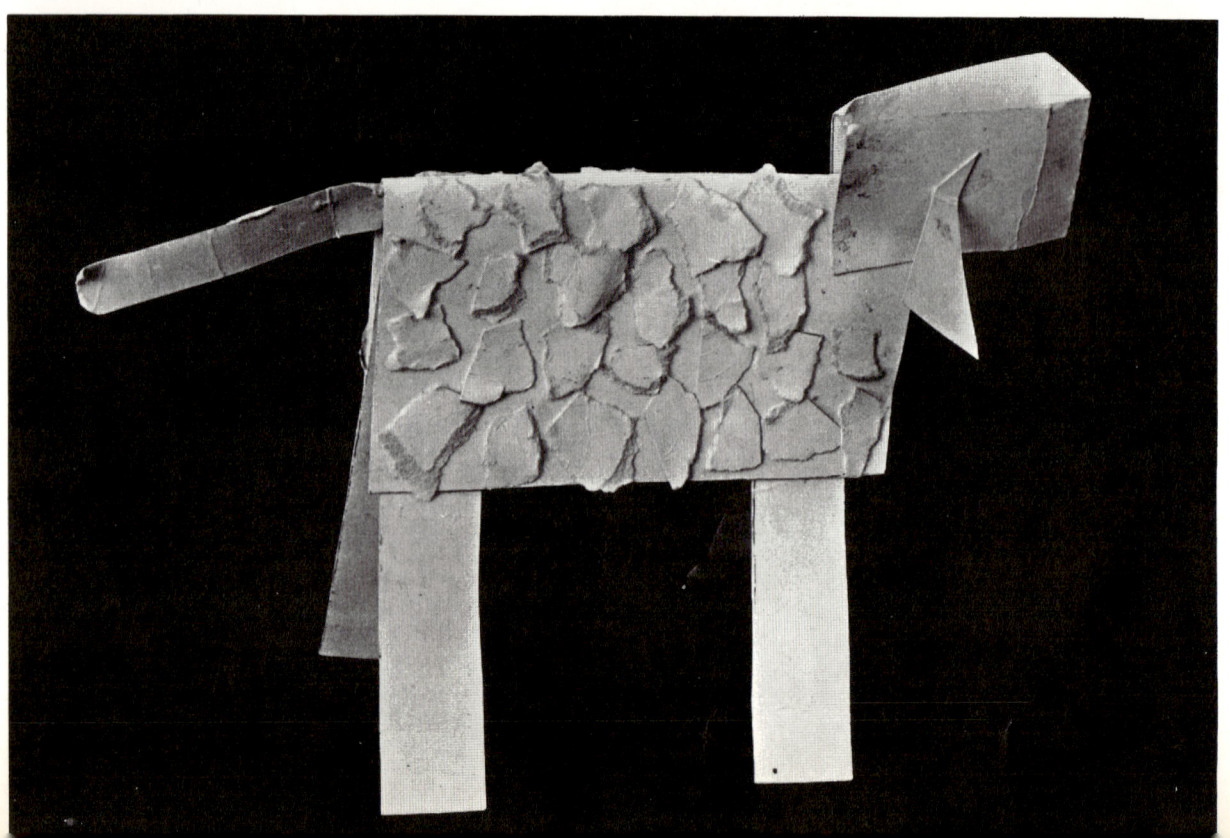

59

Here we show how a group of six trees has been produced by ink-rolling the original two tree cut-card design. In order to create the texture of the ground, a rolled impression of a very coarse glass-paper was taken after the trees had been completed. A whole forest of trees could be developed in this way, for use as a frieze, mural or backcloth.

Here fringes and curls of paper and card have been used to help increase the richness of the textures. The result has a more three-dimensional effect than the earlier examples.

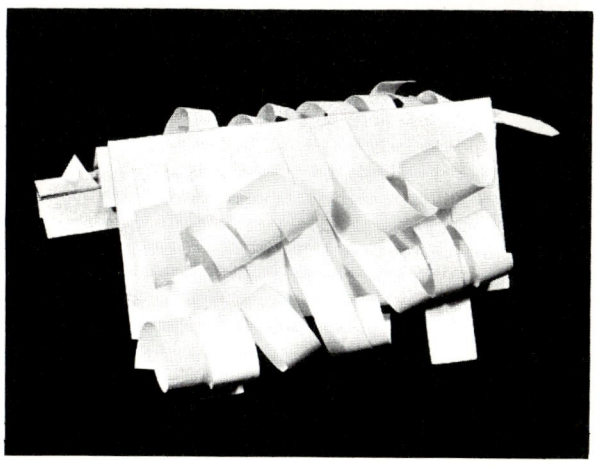

62

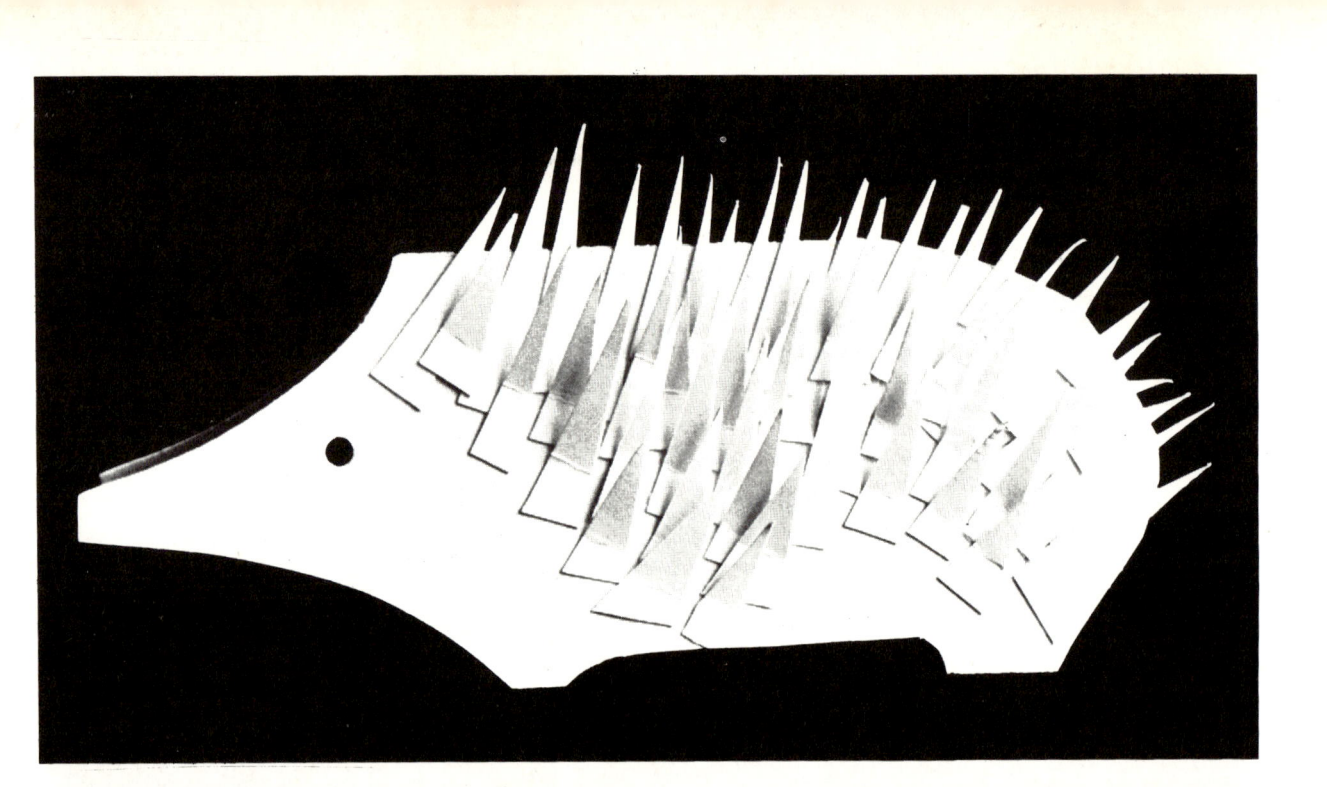

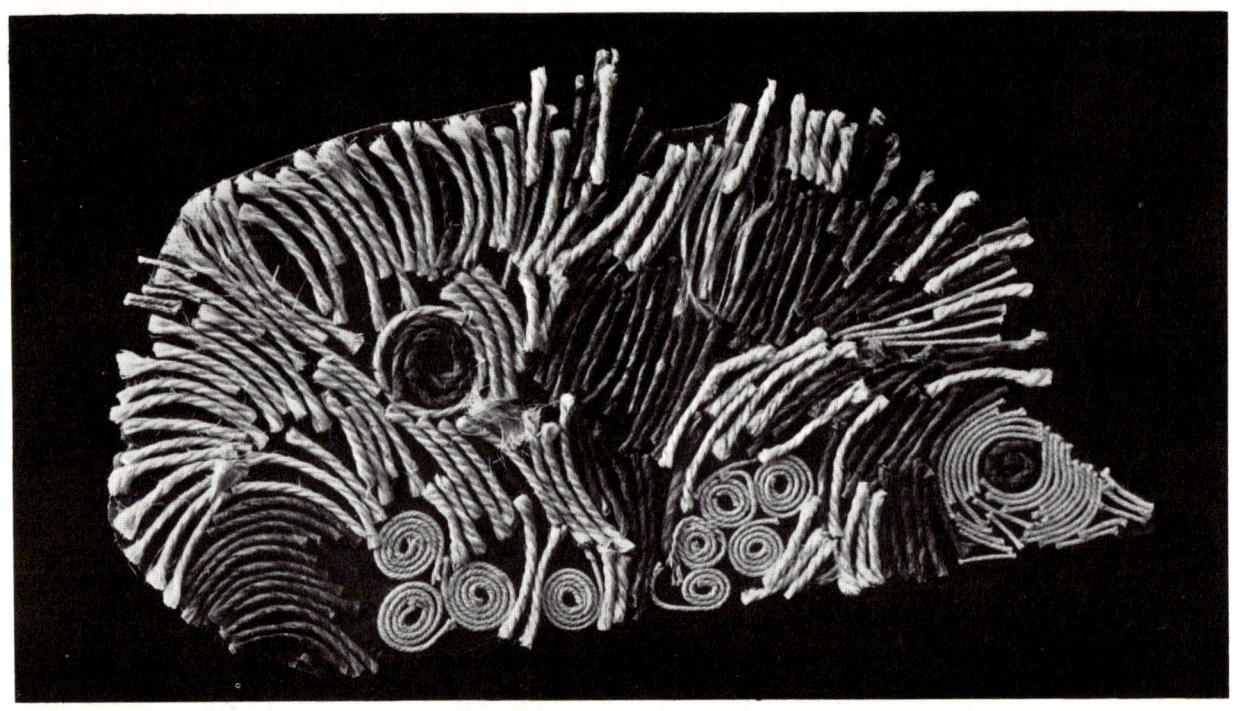

In the figure of the hedgehog the triangular spines were not glued completely flat, but allowed to stand out to give a high-relief effect.

The second hedgehog uses different types of string in various ways to create a low-relief surface. Provided reasonably strong card has been used to prevent too much buckling, designs like the string hedgehog or any other models made of non-white materials can always be sprayed or painted white, if you want an all-white project.

You can also link the constructional techniques we have described with other materials which offer their own individual possibilities. Thus the cat is covered with straw fur from packaging waste, with just a touch of drawing on the features, and the pig shows how a section from an old egg-crate can make quite a plausible head.

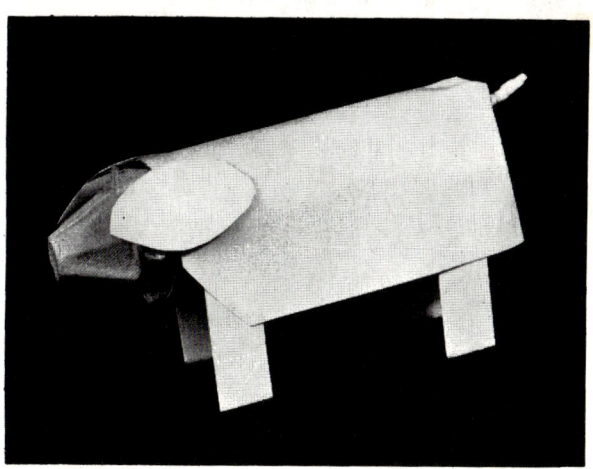

Cut Coloured Paper

It would be a pity if we were always to deprive children of the enjoyment of using colour, once they have reached a certain stage with their models. There is something very attractive about the clear-cut, positive appearance of pieces of coloured paper which have been carefully arranged and glued down. They have the advantage that they can be assembled in a variety of ways until they are just right, and then secured with gum or glue. Although matt papers are in many ways very pleasant they are easily marked by greasy fingers and so it is probably better to use a glossy finish, especially with young children. Apart from the normal sources such as stationers and art and craft material suppliers, you can again resort to the waste-box and cut up scraps, old posters and notices, particularly any with unusual colours, such as those in the fluorescent range.

Let us now look at the ways in which cut and torn coloured paper can enhance even the most simple designs. Illustrated are a selection of mobiles which use basic shapes of white, coloured, metallic and fluorescent paper and card. The first mobile consists simply of rectangular cuts of card. These were laid flat on a table and a piece of thread placed across them and attached to the pieces by glueing some parts of the decorations over the top. This simple style of mobile is easier to make than the cantilever type, which can sometimes be rather difficult to balance.

The mobile suspended from a hoop of wire used the slotted technique. Wooden hoops, bars, coat-hangars, crosses and even old umbrella frames can be used to hang mobiles from, and it is a good idea to suspend them somewhere draughty so that the pieces rotate easily.

Another mobile illustrates the technique of folding a piece of paper several times, cutting into the folds, and then opening it out to reveal a decorative doily or snowflake design. Other examples show the slotted technique.

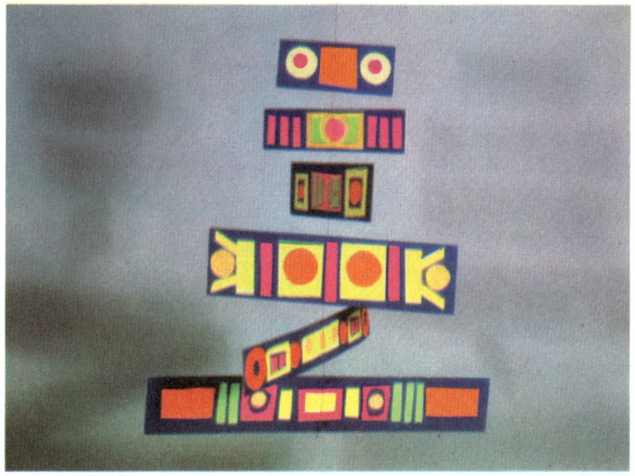

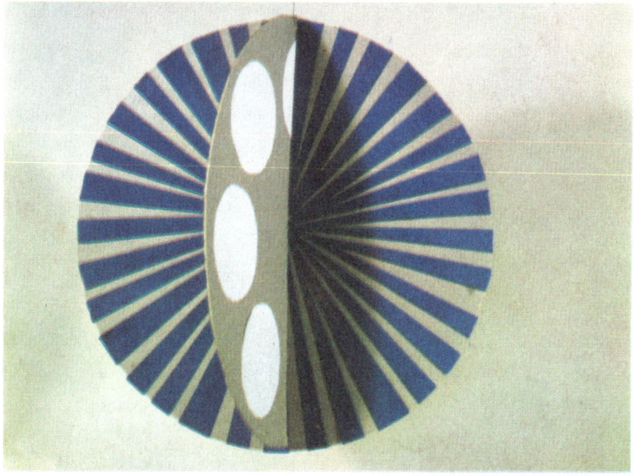

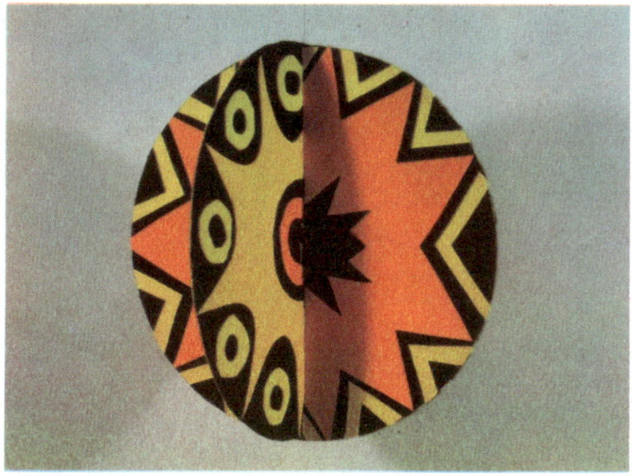

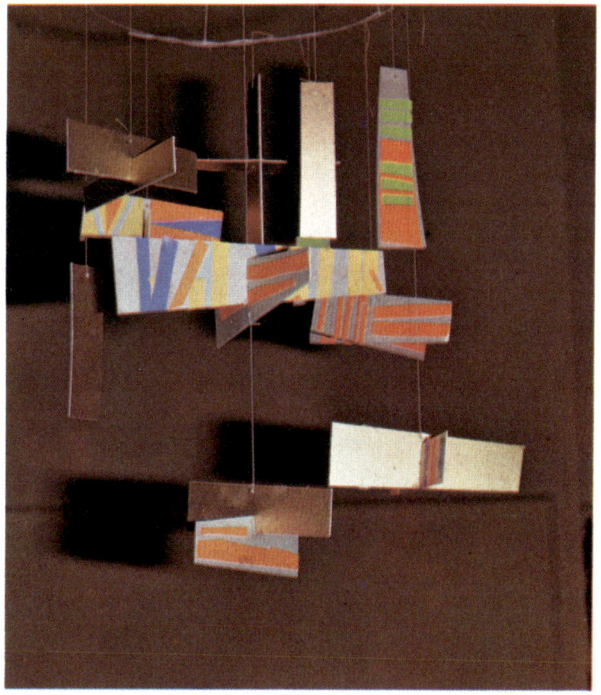

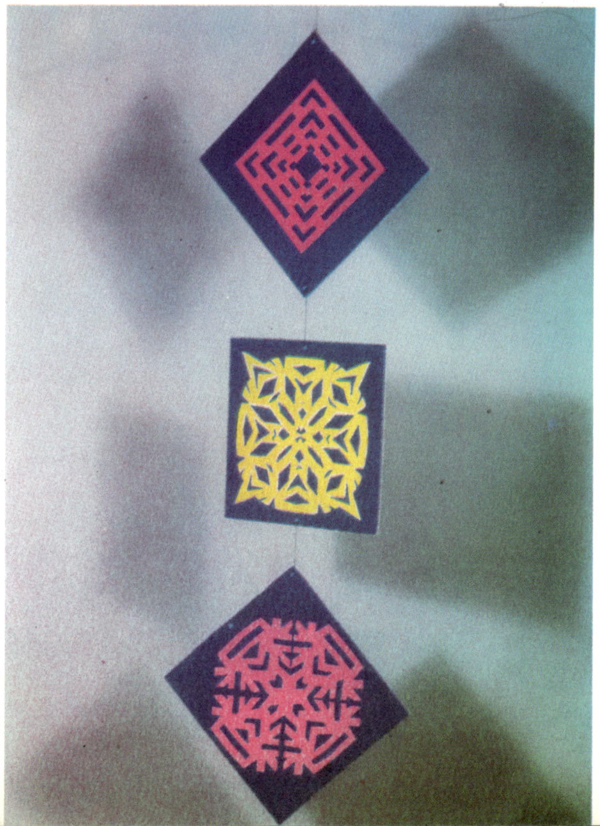

The techniques described in this book are particularly suitable for making models for festive occasions. To prove our point, here are a group of ideas which have been devised with Christmas in mind.

First some Christmas trees. The circular motifs were printed with bottle-tops dipped in paint. One set of trees was sprayed with paint and then decorated with brightly coloured cut-outs of paper.

The angels didn't really need any colour, but these items are particularly eye-catching because of their bold brilliance.

67

68

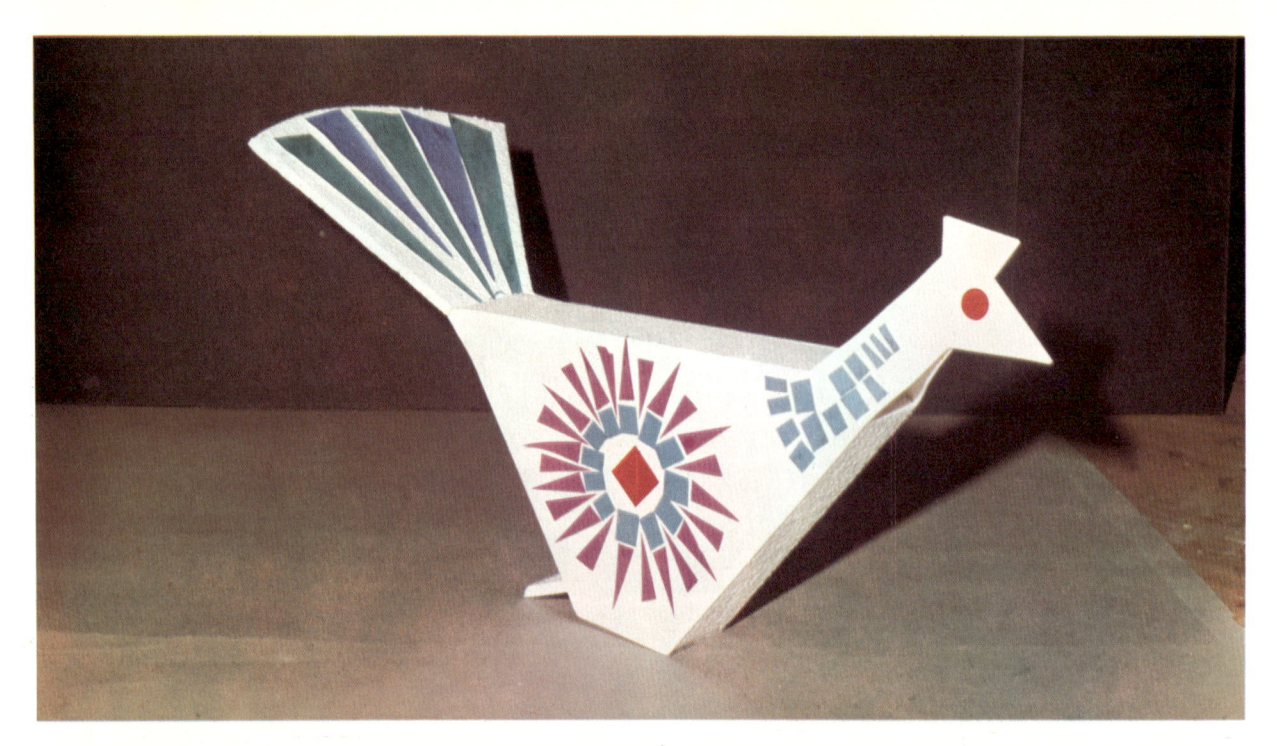

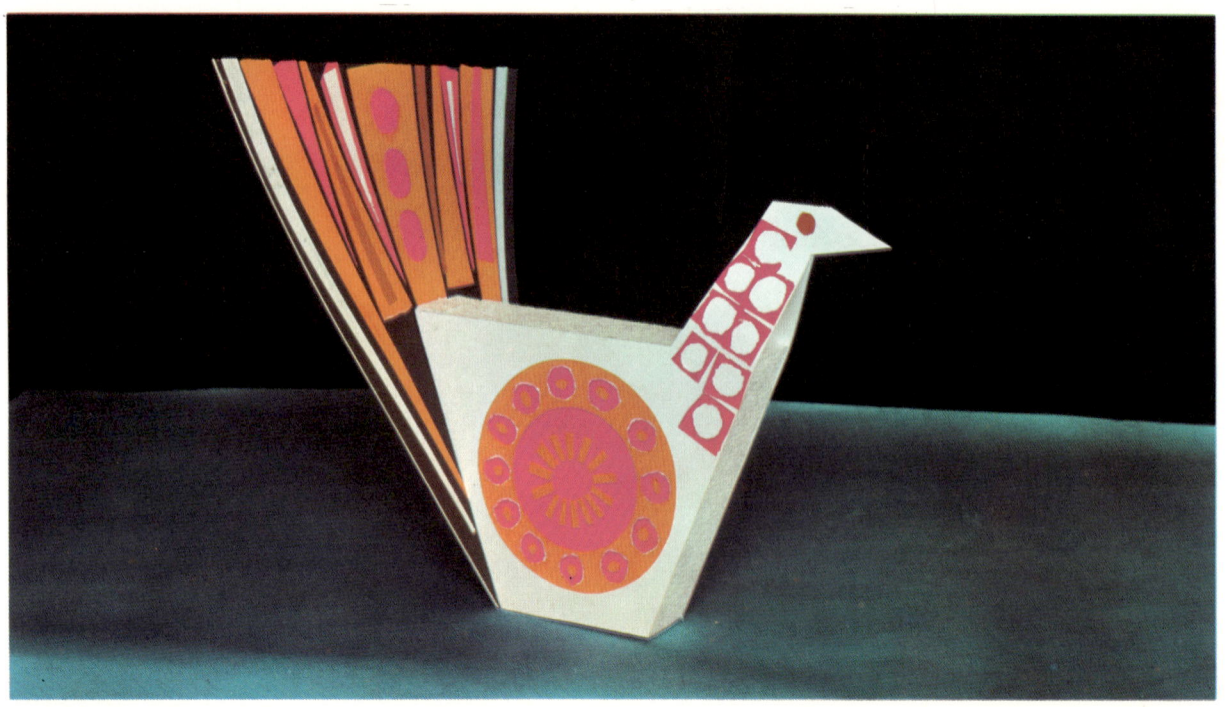

Here are some attractive and colourful variations on the theme of birds and their tails. In the top two, polystyrene tile strips have been used to fill out the birds' bodies. Notice how the decoration on the neck of the red and orange bird makes use of the pieces left over when the red circles on the body were cut out.

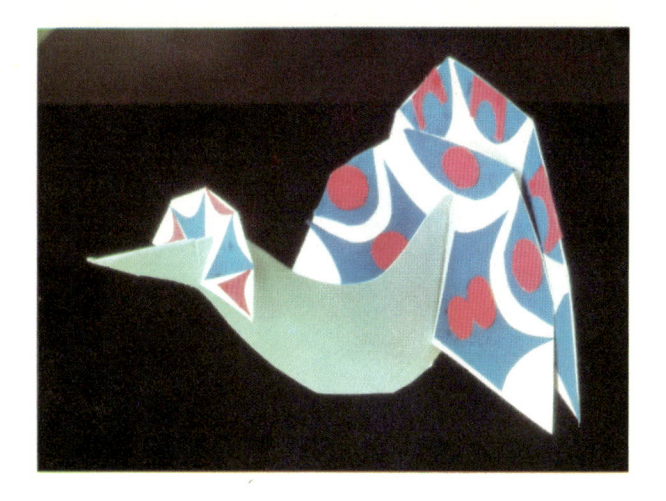

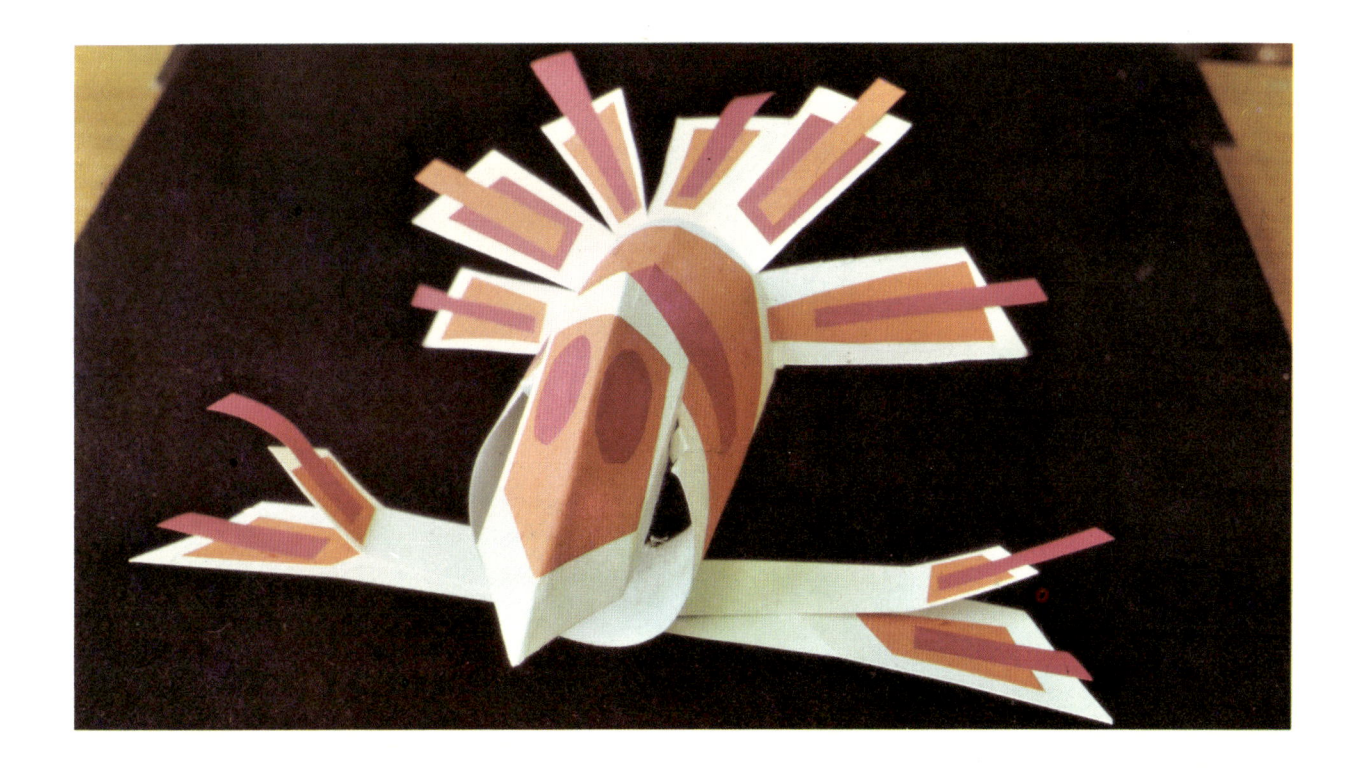

70

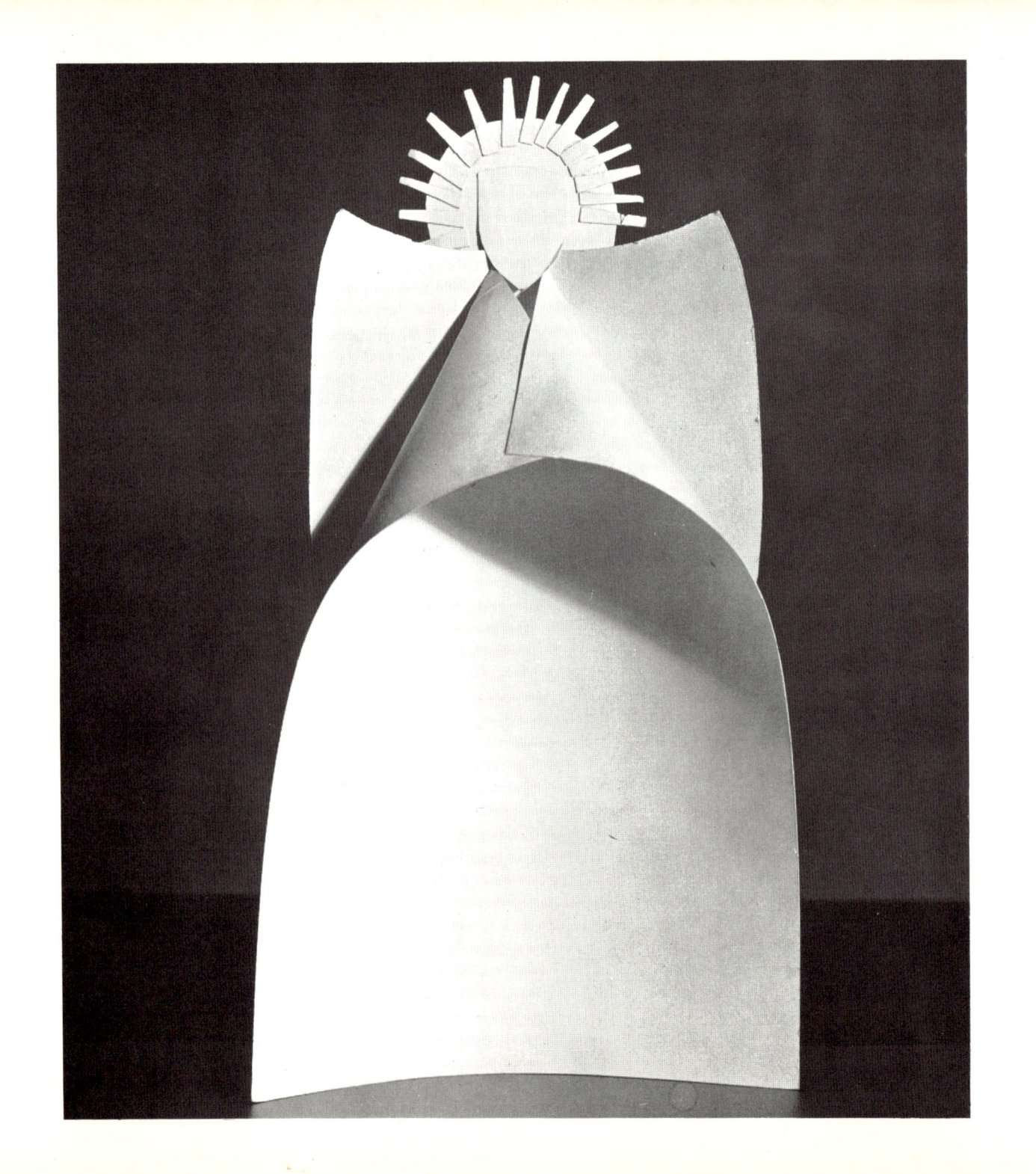

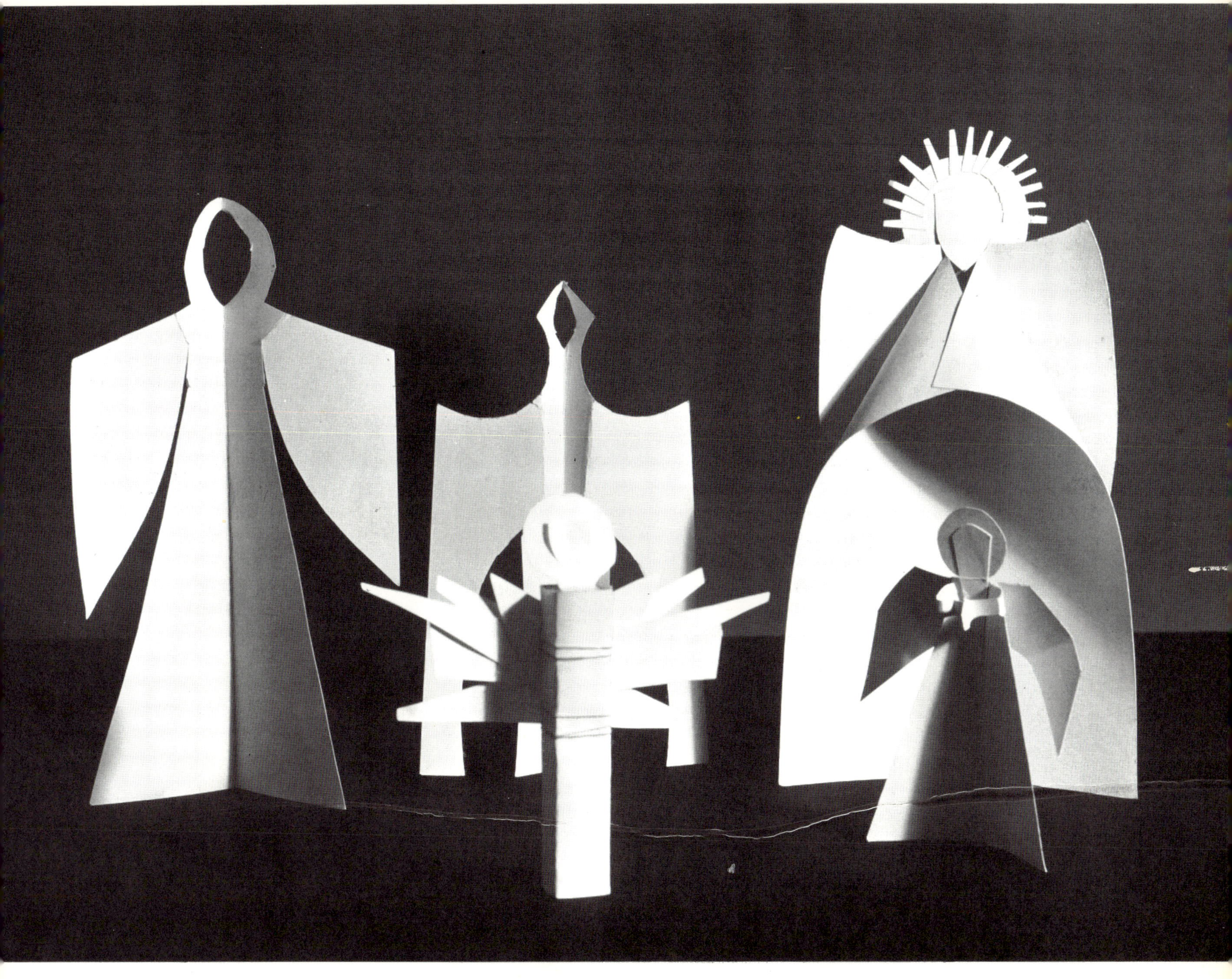

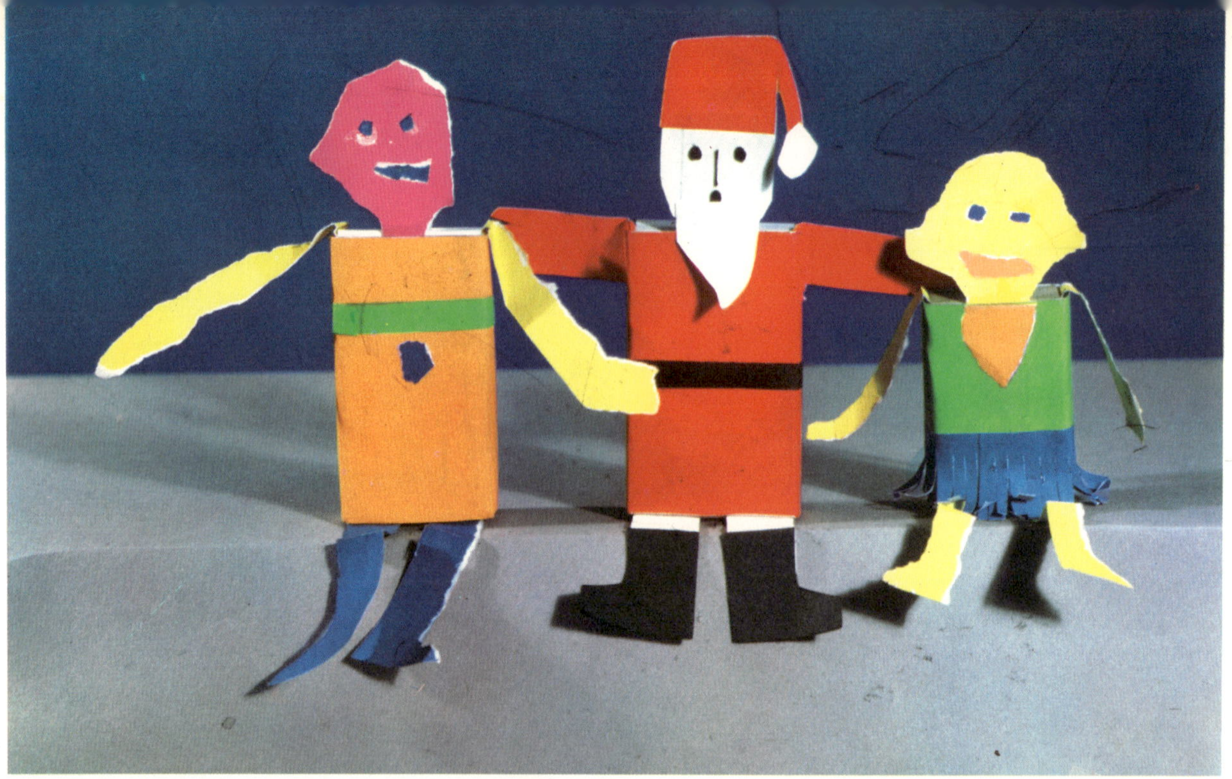

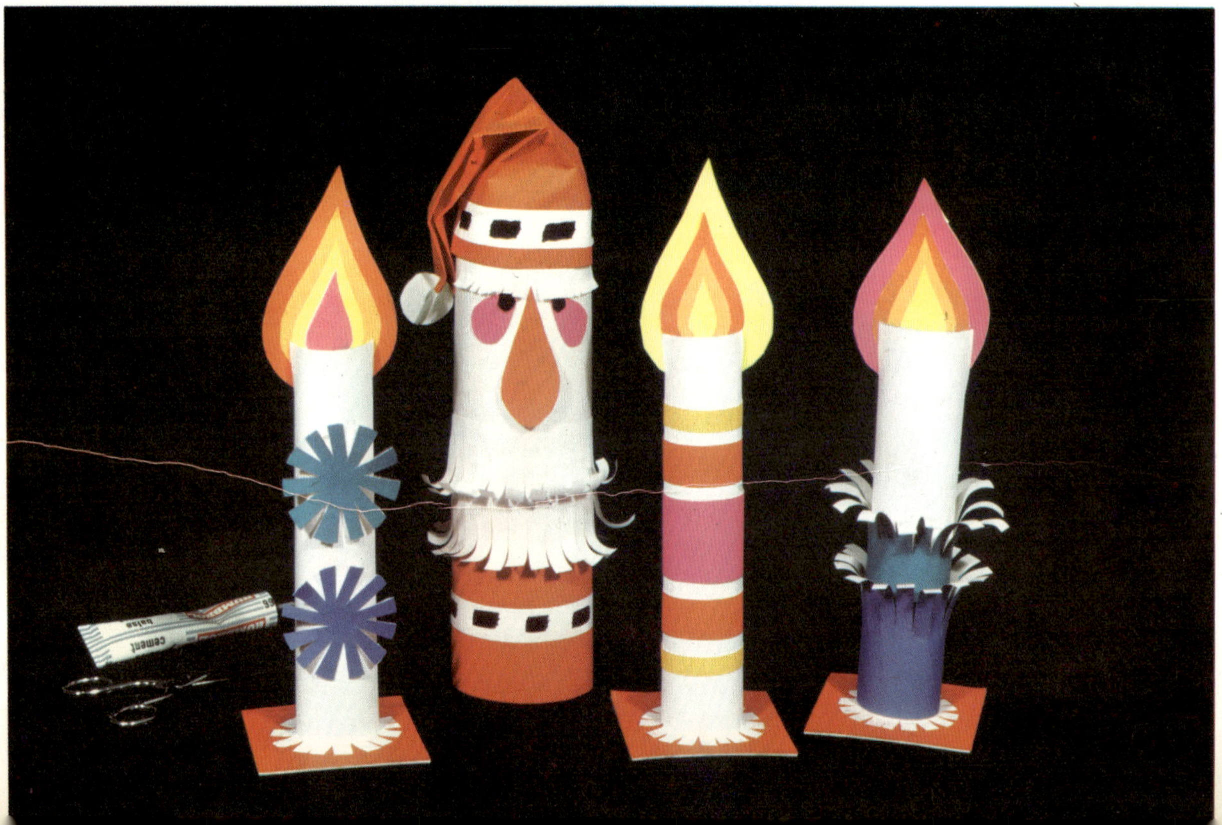
cement

The little group of figures used matchboxes and cigarette packets for the bodies, which were then wrapped and decorated with cut and torn paper.

The ship bears paper shields which were rubbed with wax crayons over a decorative relief-design. They were then pasted on to card discs and mounted on the side of the ship. It is a great help when building a ship to fix at least two supporting struts or deck brackets inside the boat, so that the masts can be securely fastened.

Apart from various kinds of opaque coloured paper you can use other materials for decoration. Mention was made earlier of the uses of a flannelgraph, which involves arranging pieces of felt on a board covered with felt. As you can place the felt board in a vertical position, it is ideal for testing ideas. The fish shows the kind of effect that can be achieved.

Coloured tissue paper is also a very interesting material to work with, especially if you take advantage of the deeper tones and changes of colour which occur when pieces are laid over each other. You need to take extra care when pasting or glueing, and we have found that rubber adhesives such as Cowgum or Studiogum are suitable, especially if used with a spreader. You can also use cellulose paste, but take care to avoid the colour coming off the damp tissue paper. The tree design shows the effectiveness of overlapping.

75

76

Crayons, Paints and Inks

In comparison with the deliberate cutting and glueing of pieces of coloured paper, drawing, painting and printing materials can be used in a much more spontaneous way and are often even more effective.

Nowadays an excellent range of graphic products is available in dozens of exciting colours. If you are using pastels, chalks or charcoal, it is advisable to spray your work with fixative to prevent it smudging.

The best drawing materials are probably wax and oil crayons and felt-tipped pens. Crayons are normally pleasant to work with and have the advantage that you can use them as a 'wax resist' and work over them with coloured inks and paints. You can also scratch or scrape patterns and textures in sgraffito fashion.

The two snakes and the circular fan all use wax and oil crayons, and the elephant has been developed with a process involving repeated candle-wax markings and layers of watercolour.

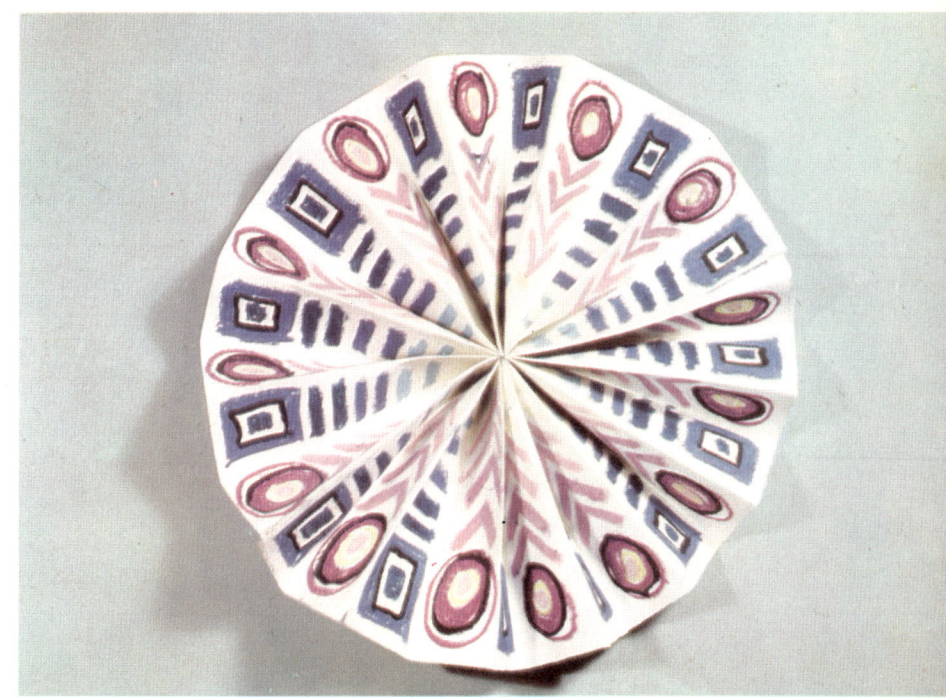

Illustrated below is a folded gecko or lizard which was decorated with different sizes of pen nibs and black Indian ink.

The other three models were made by a ten-year-old boy, who used ordinary pencil to shade in some of the form of the creatures and to define their arms and legs a little more.

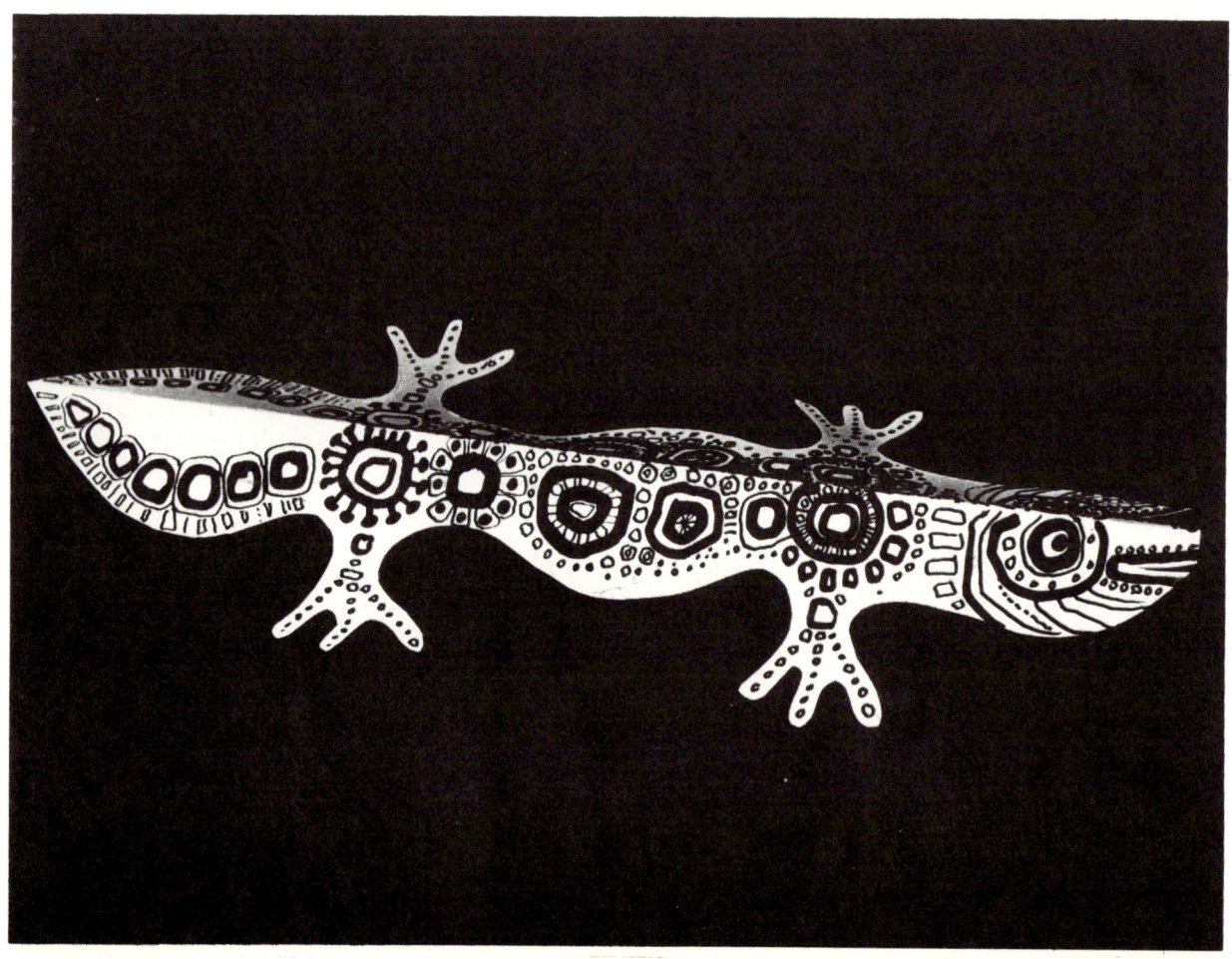

Paint can be laid on with a sponge, rags, screwed-up paper or other materials, and this entails a 'printing-down' procedure. You can use a variety of implements such as potato-pieces, bottle-tops, corks, edges of card, wood, lino etc. In fact you can use any method you like as long as the result is really what you want.

Both the camel and the giraffe have printed-down decoration. The camel also has coloured paper strips.

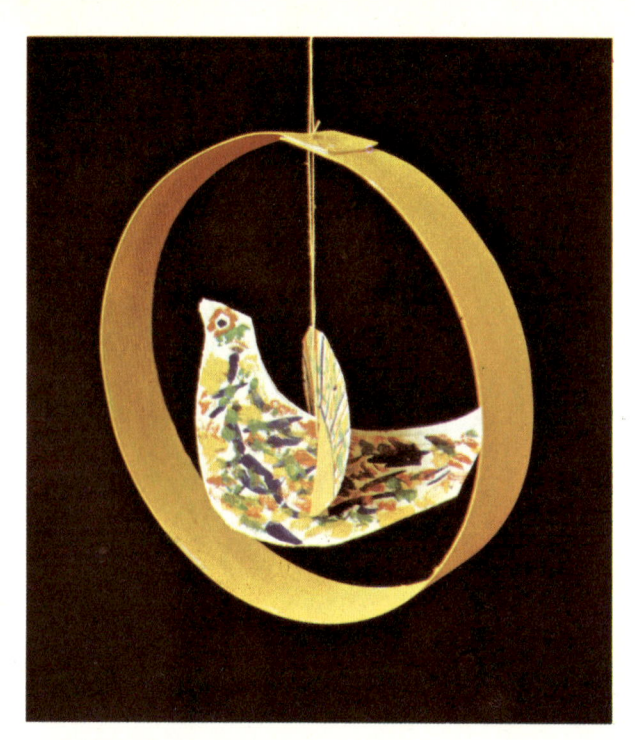

The owl is a good example of potato-printing; in this case it was printed with fairly thick, opaque paint on black sugar paper. (Coloured paper and cards will often produce a characteristic quality when used as a background. Here the over-printing of the owl's feathers gives some indication of the effects that can be obtained.)

In the two birds, watercolour and poster-colours have been painted on thinly in the one case and thickly on the mobile bird. Colour was dabbed on to the king's head with the fingers, and applied to the rhinoceros with a sponge.

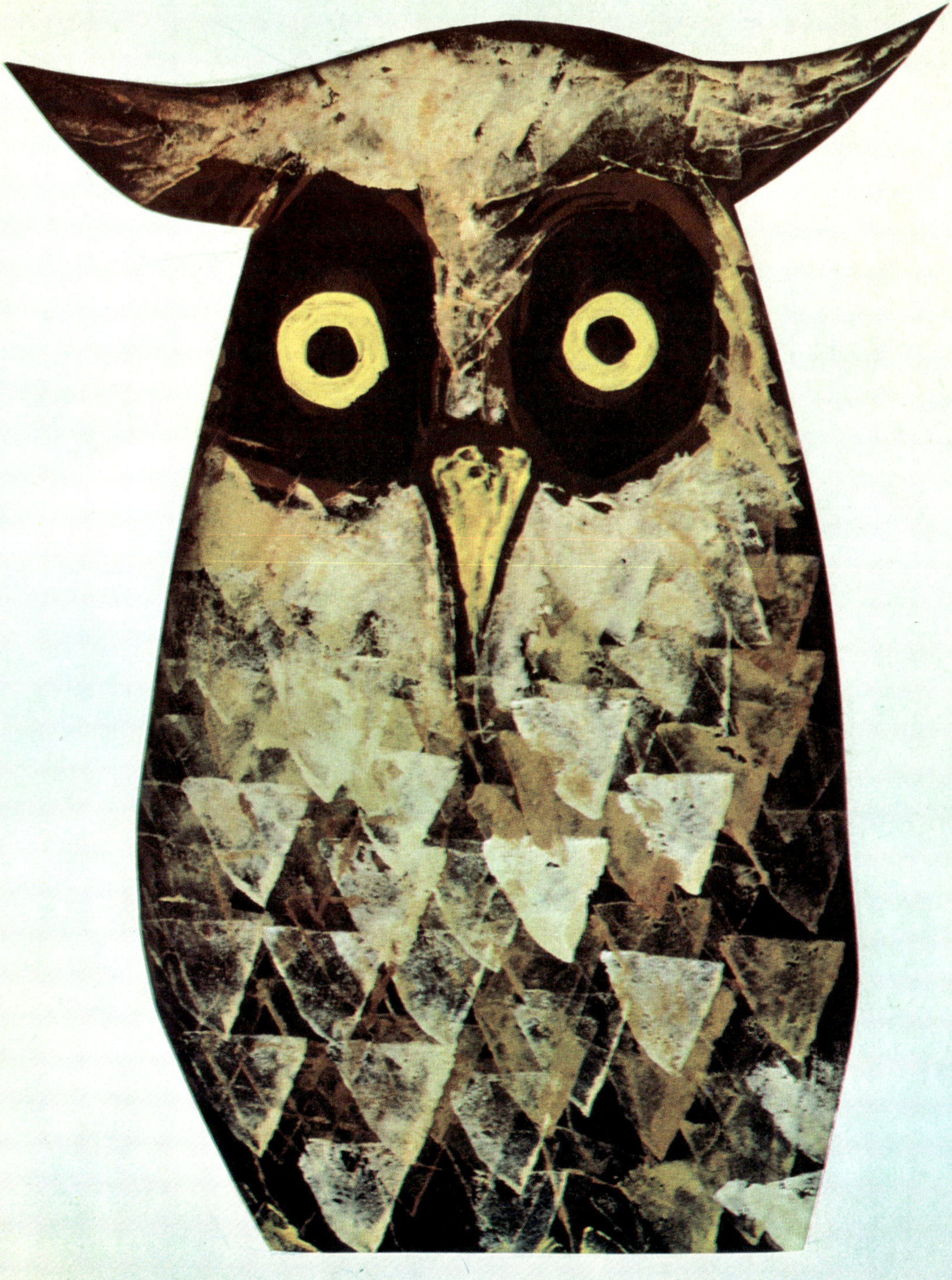

86

87

88

In forming the tree, various shapes of brush were used with coloured inks and pressed down to reveal the actual form of each brush stroke. You will notice that there is a graduation of tones in many of the individual strokes.

Black ink was used once again on this fish, and if you look closely you will see that pieces of card, corks and bottle-tops were used to print down the ink. The glowing effect of coloured inks can be seen in the colour photograph on page 89, which shows the final stage in this fish design.

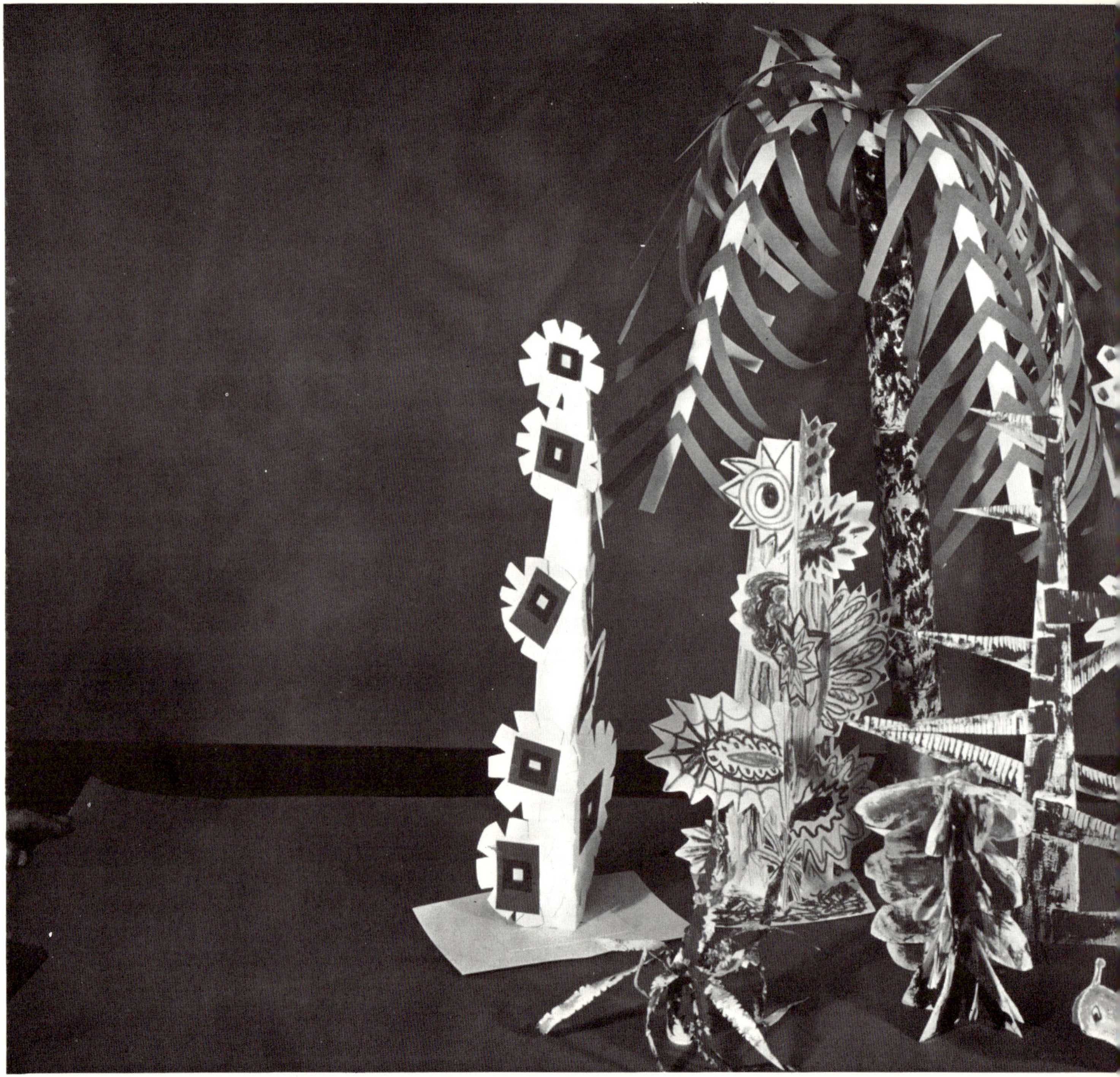

If you assemble examples of the different techniques of construction together, you will see the great potentiality of the various kinds of models.

Primary schoolteachers produced the models for the three scenes of the group of trees, the village square and the village wedding. They show that it is possible for a number of people to work together as a team on a particular assignment. In the case of the wedding, the individual pieces were constructed separately, without the idea of a group project, which is why there is a lack of co-ordination in the scale and proportion. But even so, the units have been formed together to make a fairly convincing scene.

92

93

In conclusion, we would like to point out that although most of the contents of this book were developed over a long period through work carried out in schools, colleges and professional, in-service and other courses, we have not yet exhausted all the possibilities. Children, teachers and private individuals will be able to discover many more for themselves, and children, in particular, naturally evolve forms of symbolism and schemata to suit their own personalities and age-groups.

If our suggestions are to succeed, it is vitally important to encourage and develop the freedom to create naturally and spontaneously. It was with this philosophy in mind that the work shown in each illustration was produced.